NORTH YORK MOORS

WEST AND SOUTH AREA

WALKS FOR MOTORISTS

Douglas Cossar
and
Geoffrey White

30 Walks with sketch maps

COUNTRYSIDE BOOKS
NEWBURY, BERKSHIRE

Countryside Books' walking guides cover most areas of England and Wales and include the following series:

County Rambles
Walks For Motorists
Exploring Long Distance Paths
Literary Walks
Pub Walks

A complete list is available from the publishers.

First published 1973
by Frederick Warne Ltd

This completely revised and updated edition
published 1992

© Douglas Cossar 1992

COUNTRYSIDE BOOKS
3 Catherine Road
Newbury, Berkshire

ISBN 1 85306 178 6

Cover photograph of Kilburn White Horse taken by Bill Meadows

Publishers' Note
At the time of publication all footpaths used in these walks were
designated as official footpaths or rights of way, but it should be borne in
mind that diversion orders may be made from time to time.
Although every care has been taken in the preparation of this Guide,
neither the Author nor the Publisher can accept responsibility for those
who stray from the Rights of Way.

Produced through MRM Associates Ltd., Reading
Typeset by Paragon Typesetters, Sandycroft, Chester
Printed in England by J. W. Arrowsmith Ltd., Bristol

Contents

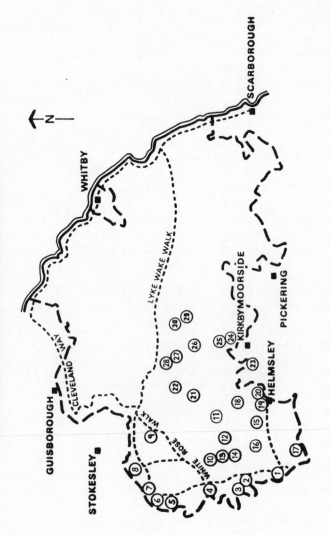

NORTH YORK MOORS NATIONAL PARK

– – – NATIONAL PARK BOUNDARY

NUMBERS DENOTE WALK START POINTS

Preface

I was delighted to be invited to prepare this revision of Geoffrey White's two volumes of *North York Moors Walks for Motorists,* one of the earliest collections of rambles for this area and one to which I myself owe many hours of pleasure.

Since 1973, when they were first published, many things have changed, so that I have found myself altering much more of the original walks than I had at first intended. The volume of traffic visiting the Moors has increased, so that walking on minor roads is now less pleasant than it was 20 years ago, and whereas to park one's car on a roadside verge was normal then, now one would prefer a recognised car park. Through lack of usage some moorland paths have all but disappeared, whereas other routes are now popular and clear. Believing that the audience for these volumes will be largely ordinary families with children and perhaps not too much experience of 'serious' walking, I have tried only to include routes where difficulties of terrain or route-finding will not interfere with the pleasure of the walking. These and other reasons make the present volumes different in many ways from their predecessors, but I hope they will be felt to be worthy successors.

All the routes are on rights of way or permissive paths (particularly through Forestry Commission plantations) or on paths where access has traditionally not been disputed. Please let me know through the publishers of any problems you may encounter.

Douglas Cossar
April 1992

Introduction

The North York Moors are a well-defined area of upland, roughly 60 kilometres from west to east and 40 from north to south, bounded on the east by the North Sea, on the north and west by the steep escarpments of the Cleveland and Hambleton Hills and on the south by the gentler dip slopes of the tabular hills. The area is dissected by a number of south-flowing streams draining into the Derwent, which flows into the Ouse, and in the north the Esk flows east to reach the sea at Whitby, being joined from the south by smaller becks.

Most of the moorland is sandstone, with occasional caps of gritstone on the highest hills. To the south these rocks are overlaid with corallian limestone, forming the tabular hills, flat-topped with a scarp to the north and gentler slopes to the south. Among the sandstone strata are thin seams of poor-quality coal, and earlier rocks below contain deposits of iron ore, jet and alum, all of which have been exploited by man, most fully in the 19th century.

The infertile soils on the sandstone now form the largest continuous area of heather moorland in England, with land use restricted to sheep pasture and grouse shooting, but arable crops are grown on the limestone plateau and there is dairy farming in the valley bottoms. Since 1920 the Forestry Commission have added extensive plantations, mainly of conifers, to the remains of the earlier deciduous forest.

The hand of man is everywhere visible, from the many Bronze Age burial mounds through the medieval monasteries and crosses to the relics of industrial activity and the delightful stone-built, red pantile roofed villages and farmsteads of today.

All this variety makes the North York Moors into a paradise for walkers, naturalists, photographers, archaeologists, historians and many others. I have tried in the rambles to provide a reasonable selection of the various delights the area has to offer, in the hope that they will be a springboard for many more expeditions of independent exploration.

The best general map of the area is probably the Ordnance Survey's Touring Map No 2 at a scale of 1" to the mile, but for the walker the essential maps are the Ordnance Survey's Outdoor Leisure Maps Nos 26 and 27 at a scale of 1:25,000; all the walks in this volume are on No 26, the Western sheet, all those in volume two are on No 27, the Eastern sheet. The North York Moors National Park's information centres at Danby and Sutton Bank stock many waymarked walks leaflets as well as a large selection of other publications on the North York Moors.

The area is crossed by many long-distance paths, official and unofficial, such as the Cleveland Way, A Wainwright's Coast to Coast Walk, the Lyke Wake Walk, the Derwent Way, the Crosses Walk, the White Rose

Walk, the Bilsland Circuit, the Eskdale Way and the Esk Valley Walk, details of which can be obtained from the information centres.

As you walk, please remember the Country Code:

Enjoy the countryside and respect its life and work.
Guard against fire risks.
Fasten all gates.
Keep dogs under control.
Keep to public paths across farm land.
Use gates and stiles to cross fences, hedges and walls.
Leave livestock, crops and machinery alone.
Take your litter home.
Help to keep all water clean.
Protect wild life, plants and trees.
Take special care on country roads.
Make no unnecessary noise.

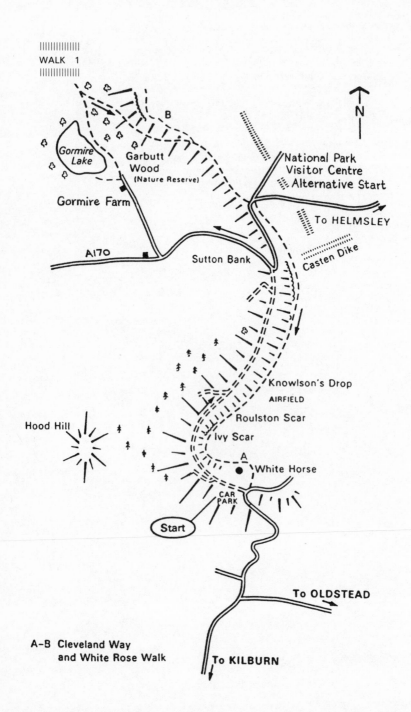

WALK 1

N

B

Gormire
Lake

Garbutt
Wood
(Nature Reserve)

Gormire Farm

National Park
Visitor Centre
Alternative Start

To HELMSLEY

A170

Sutton Bank

Casten Dike

Knowlson's Drop

AIRFIELD

Roulston Scar

Hood Hill

Ivy Scar

A

White Horse

CAR
PARK

Start

To OLDSTEAD

A-B Cleveland Way
and White Rose Walk

To KILBURN

WHITE HORSE AND GRAND CIRCLE ROUTE TO GORMIRE

WALK 1

★

6 miles (9.5 km)

The beauty of this excursion is that it combines some lovely corners under the lee of the hills with the grandeur of the cliff walk back to the starting point.

Leave your car in the free car park immediately below the Kilburn White Horse (GR 514 813). Alternatively, start from the National Park car park and information centre at the top of Sutton Bank (GR 515 830) (charge), but then you have the views from the start and not as the climax to the walk.

Leave the White Horse car park at the far side opposite the entrance by passing round the right-hand of the two locked barriers into the forest on a very clear path. Where there are forks keep right, under the cliff, of which there are some impressive views, until you reach a fork with a notice between the two branches saying 'Forestry Commission No Riding Please', where you must keep left on the lower, slightly wider path (the right-hand branch ascends and passes a bench). The green track has much of interest to the botanist, and gliders may well be observed above, making use of the upward air currents. The track emerges onto the hairpin bend of a rough gravel track: bear right here, to reach the hairpin bend on the main road on Sutton Bank. Turn left downhill. There is a ten minute road walk so take care.

At the foot of the hill turn right on the bridle road 50 yards before a white house, and breathe deeply to get rid of the exhaust fumes. Pass to the right of Gormire Farm and through the gate into Garbutt Wood Nature Reserve. In a few yards fork right on the narrower path, which soon brings you quite close to the peaceful Gormire Lake. Gormire's waters seem seldom to be ruffled except by the occasional passing of moorhen or duck or the rising of the fish. Keep forward on the clear path, soon leaving the lake below on your left. Shortly after coming close to the left-hand edge of the wood a board-walk leads you safely across a wet section.

Where the board-walk ends and you reach a broad track descending left, turn sharp right on a narrow ascending path signposted Garbutt Wood. Shortly, by a Yorkshire Wildlife Trust sign, you come to a stile in

9

the fence on your right leading out of the wood and a notice saying 'Sloping Path'. Follow this delightful path. It coincides with part of the Garbutt Wood Nature Trail, which explains the presence of wooden posts with numbers on. Ignore a path forking left by post number 13. At post 10 you come to a set of steps on the right leading downhill towards the lake, but you fork left uphill. At post 7 you pass a massive boulder and keep left, and soon afterwards you pass a notice indicating the end of the nature reserve.

Glorious views open up to the right as you climb: on a clear day you can see as far as Great Whernside in Wharfedale, with Wensleydale further north. Gormire is below, a jewel in a perfect setting, reputed to be bottomless, and the subject of legends, such as the one of the witch chased over these cliffs by hounds who fell into the lake and came up again at a keld nine miles away.

On reaching a cross path at the top of the slope you join the Cleveland Way. Turn right and follow the edge of the escarpment to the main road at Sutton Bank. Cross this and walk forward to the direction indicator on the other side, which shows the distances to towns and features many miles away. The path continues along the top, by the edge of the airfield of the Yorkshire Gliding Club, above the cliffs known as Knowlson's Drop, Roulston Scar and Ivy Scar. Ignore a Forestry Commission path descending on the right beside a notice about the White Horse Walk. Soon you round the corner to the White Horse cut into the turf on Low Town Brow.

The best known statistic about the Horse is that 20 people can picnic on its eye! Other vital information is that, led by the Kilburn schoolmaster Mr John Hodgson, 30 people created it in 1857. The base is limestone, not chalk as with many White Horses cut into hillsides, and to be kept white it has to be covered with lime from time to time. It covers about two acres of ground; its height is 228 ft, its length 314 ft. The lovely valley below, leading to Oldstead, was cut by the meltwaters of a glacier.

A flight of steps beyond the tail of the White Horse leads down to the car park below.

BOLTBY, LITTLE MOOR AND SOUTH WOODS

WALK 2

★

5 miles (8 km)

In this book there is quite a concentration of walks on or below the western cliffs of the National Park, simply because the pronounced features of crag, woodland and foothills with valleys between make the area one of delight and tranquillity.

Boltby is reached from Thirsk via Felixkirk, a pretty village on rising ground. The road between Felixkirk and Boltby is a pleasant one, and it is worth stopping here and there for backward views across the plain. Boltby is a typical village on the fringe of the moors, built of local stone and tiles.

Drive straight through the village and out at the far end; just after a left-hand bend sign, on the bend itself, there is a largish layby on the right. Park here (GR 494 866).

Walk back down the road into the village, turning left just after the first building on the left, a former Methodist chapel, along a tarmacked lane. Ahead on the skyline you will soon see quarry workings, where there was once an aerial ropeway, and to the right of the workings are some fine whitestone cliffs, Boltby Scar. In the lane there is a ford and footbridge, and then at the end of the lane enter the field ahead and make for the top right-hand corner.

When you reach the bracken line ignore the clear path ascending left and bear slightly right (there is a waymark on the old gatepost) towards the trees, and soon a gate leads into the wood. Shortly extensive views open up over the fence on your right. The fence becomes a wall, and at a level grassy spot the path forks (there is a farm down to the right) by a public bridleway sign: take the left fork, signposted Littlemoor. Soon after reaching a fence on the left you come to a stile by a gate: cross and bear half-right over the rough pasture to a gate into the wood.

Soon you cross straight over a track and continue on the clear path uphill, which eventually leads to a gate out of the woodland. Continue forward to meet a clear cross-path. This is the Cleveland Way. It is worth making a detour to the left for a few hundred yards, not so much for the hill fort, of which few remains are visible, as for the views from the top

11

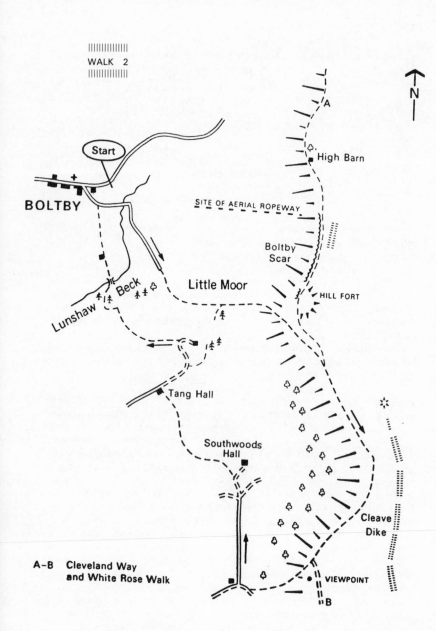

WALK 2

Start

+ BOLTBY

Lunshaw Beck

Little Moor

SITE OF AERIAL ROPEWAY

High Barn

A

Boltby Scar

HILL FORT

Tang Hall

Southwoods Hall

Cleave Dike

VIEWPOINT

B

A-B Cleveland Way
and White Rose Walk

N

12

of Boltby Scar. Then return to this point and continue on the clear path round the wide sweep of the bay. The woods below are South Woods and beyond them the large building is Southwoods Hall. At the far side of the bay the path makes a sharp turn left, and it is worth walking forward to the edge here for the views of Gormire Lake and Roulston Scar beyond.

Now retrace your steps for 200 yards to where a Cleveland Way signpost marks the start of our descent. A path forks sharply down, soon passing between rocks. At what seems to be a fork, keep right on the lower path and soon pass into Garbutt Wood by a Yorkshire Wildlife Trust Nature Reserve sign. Follow the clear path down through the wood (muddy in places); at a fork keep right (bridleway sign) — Gormire Lake can soon be glimpsed through the trees to the left — on the clear path which winds its way downhill. Nearly at the bottom it forks: keep right, continuing the descent (going left would bring you to the route of Walk 1). Join a wider track coming in from the left and keep down out of the wood.

Bear right in front of Southwoods Lodge through the gate and along a level track. Pass through another gate to a crossing of tracks and keep forward. Where the track bears right to Southwoods Hall, keep forward through the trees with the fence to your left, soon to pass through a gate, after which the grassy track bears slightly left away from the fence on the right to a gate at the left-hand corner of the wood ahead. Keep forward up the facing slope to pass to the right of a young plantation, at the top bearing right to follow the right-hand line of power cables across the field to a gate at the far side.

The track now bears left again, heading straight across the next field to the left of the house seen at the far side. Bear right when you reach the far side to pass to the right of the house (Tang Hall) and join a country lane. Turn right along it, over a cattle grid (signpost to Greendale, the farm seen ahead). The next cattle grid is electrified, so you must pass through the gate to the right of it. Then continue on the track to where it curves right to the farm, but 100 yards before it reaches the buildings fork sharply left off it along a good farm track. The track soon bears left, crosses a ditch and approaches a wood. Ignore the gate ahead and turn right along the edge of the wood to the far end, where you cross a stile by a gate (signpost to Boltby) into the wood and follow the path to the far right-hand corner of the wood, where another stile leads into a path between a fence on the right and Lunshaw Beck on the left.

Cross the footbridge and bear half-right across the field, aiming to the right of the stone barn, where you pick up a track which leads along with the hedge first to your right, then to your left. You rejoin your outward route through a gate. Turn left to return to the village, and at the main road turn right for your car.

13

STEEPLE CROSS AND BOLTBY FOREST

WALK 3

★

4 miles (6.5 km)

An easy stroll on good tracks, mainly through woodland, but with some fine views. The outward route follows the Cleveland Way, the return is on Forestry Commission tracks.

Drive east through Boltby and continue until you reach the steep (25%) gradient of Sneck Yate Bank. Pass the access roads to Hesketh Grange on the right and Low and High Paradise on the left, and just before a left-hand bend park in a layby on the right (marked as 'Quarry (dis)' on the Outdoor Leisure map) (GR 507 876). If there is no space here drive on for a short distance: a gap in the hedge on the right gives access to an area where cars are often parked; or drive up to the crossroads at the top of the hill and park at the start of the drove road on the left.

From the old quarry walk uphill for a few yards to where a gate on the left gives access to the forest (Cleveland Way sign). Follow the track, which can be muddy for short stretches, through the wood. After passing through a gate you are in more open woodland with extensive views left. Join a narrow tarmacked road and bear right up it. At a fork keep right (on the road) up to High Paradise Farm (refreshments available in the summer). The track, now no longer tarmacked, leads to the left of the farm, to join the Hambleton Drove Road at a T junction. Turn left along it, noticing how wide it is between its enclosing walls.

A gate leads into the forest. Keep forward on the track, to emerge from the forest again at another gate. Over it on the right you can see the stump of Steeple Cross. But do not pass through the gate. Instead leave the Cleveland Way and take the Forestry Commission road on the left a few yards before it (a notice says 'No Admission to Vehicles'). In 100 yards where the track splits into three, take the left branch. While the trees on the right are still young there are fine views across to the Pennines. Take the first track on the right, slanting sharply back and downhill. At the T junction at the foot of the hill you really want to go straight over, but your way is barred by a fence. But go right for a few yards to the end of the fence, pass round it and return to continue your downward route.

In a few yards you meet another forest road where you bear left. Descend gently to a T junction and turn right. At the next fork keep left

14

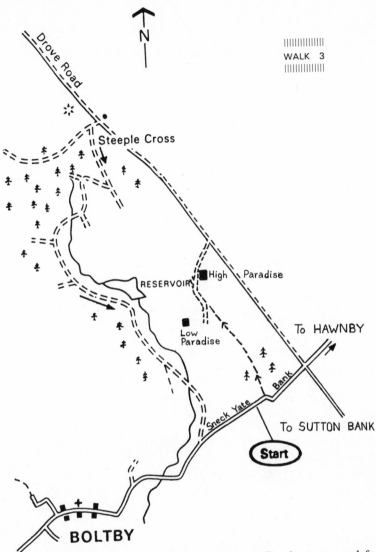

on the slightly descending road. Soon you have a valley down to your left. At the next junction bear left. Soon look out for Boltby Reservoir through the trees on the left. Having passed the reservoir, ignore the track on the left going down to it and keep forward on the forest road. At a fork keep left on the main forest road, descending close to the edge of the wood on the left. Eventually the road crosses the stream (Lunshaw Beck) and climbs to join the motor road. Turn left up this to return to the car.

15

||||||||||||||
WALK 4
||||||||||||||

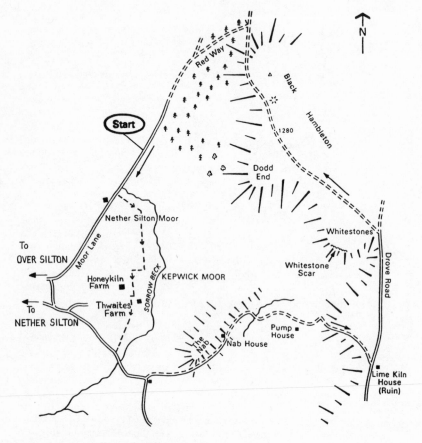

Red Way

Black

Hambleton

1280

Start

Dodd
End

Nether Silton Moor

Whitestones

Moor Lane

Whitestone
Scar

To
OVER SILTON

Honeykiln
Farm

KEPWICK MOOR

Drove Road

SORROW BECK

To
NETHER SILTON

Thwaites
Farm

Pump
House

The Nab

Nab House

Lime Kiln
House
(Ruin)

N

KEPWICK

THE DROVE ROAD OVER BLACK HAMBLETON

WALK 4

★

6½ miles (10.5 km)

The history of the old drovers' roads, used extensively to take cattle from Scotland to the south in the 17th and 18th centuries, makes an interesting study. One of the most romantic existed long before the Romans came; the drovers passing through Yarm on the way to Malton and York made full use of the high level route which entered the Clevelands at Scarth Nick, passed over the top (or nearly the top) of Black Hambleton and continued to the region above Sutton Bank and beyond. From the point of view of the walker, undoubtedly the best part of the road is that over Black Hambleton and round the top edge of the bay overlooking the Siltons and Kepwick.

The starting point of today's walk is the Forestry Commission's Silton picnic area. Over Silton and Nether Silton are signposted from the A19 Thirsk to Teesside road about 7 miles north of Thirsk. After leaving Nether Silton on the road to Kepwick take the first turn left (signposted Over Silton) and turn right into a no through road after 200 yards; coming from Over Silton in the direction of Kepwick, the no through road is on the left. Drive up it until the tarmac ends and the forest begins. Here on the left is the picnic area (GR 467 937).

Leave the picnic site and turn right, following the road you have just driven along until you are 200 yards before Hunter's Hill Farm on the right, where the road passes through a gateway (there is a caravan over the hedge on the left). Go through the large gate on the left (yellow waymark) and walk straight across the field to another gate at the far side. The bulk of Black Hambleton dominates to the left. Pass through the gate and keep on across the next field to a stile at the far side. The route of the right of way has now been diverted, so the next section may not correspond to your OS map. Cross the stile and turn right, walking at an angle of about 40° to the hedge on your right, to a large gate. Continue forward with a hedge to your left. At the end of the field turn right, still with the hedge to your left, but when you come to a stile in this hedge cross it and continue forward still with a hedge to your left. Honeykiln Farm is 100 yards to your right.

17

Towards the end of this field bear right to cut the corner, then bear left again along the hedge for a few yards to the corner where there should be a stile. Keep on with the hedge to your left (Thwaites Farm is to your left) to a stile in the corner of the field. Cross the farm access road diagonally right to another stile and again follow a hedge to your left through this field and the two following ones. Cross the footbridge and bear slightly right over a large field to a white gate in the opposite hedge.

Turn left along the road, which soon makes a sharp turn to the left, followed in 250 yards by a sharp one to the right. But on this second bend keep straight ahead up the access road to Nab Farm. At the farm the track passes to the right of all the buildings, through a gate, and continues across the middle of the next field, passing to the left of a stone wall and then bearing right to a bridge over a stream. Now leave the main track for a less clear one curving left up to a gate in a wall, beyond which is an old but well constructed limekiln. The clear, ascending track soon picks up a wall on the right, which it follows all the way to the summit ridge. The Drove Road is reached through a gate at the top, at the site of the ruined Lime Kiln House.

Turn left on the wide green expanse between walls and enjoy walking on the springy turf. At Whitestones — White Gill Head — 50 yards after the wall on your left makes a sharp turn left, the track forks: take the left fork, soon to pick up the wall again. The view to the north opens out as you reach the top of the hill. Eventually the track descends steeply off Black Hambleton and comes near to the conifers which will have been seen on the left for some little time. Before coming to the end of the trees look for a gate on the left (bridleway sign to Nether Silton) leading to a grassy ride through the forest. It can be quite wet, but conditions soon improve when you reach a well-made forest road. Turn left along this and follow it down, ignoring minor tracks to left and right and at one point another well-made forest road branching right, all the way back to the car.

SILTON MOOR, THIMBLEBY BANK AND OAK DALE

WALK 5

★

7½ miles (12 km)

Take the Hawnby road out of Osmotherley and at the end of the village fork left, again signposted to Hawnby. Follow the road, which climbs to Thimbleby Moor, until it makes a sharp turn left by a large parking place (GR 479 959). The walk starts here. (An alternative starting point would be the Forestry Commission's Silton picnic site — see the directions for Walk 4.)

Follow the old Drove Road, the broad track signposted Cleveland Way, Sneck Yate, towards the bulk of Black Hambleton. Ignore the first track forking right and keep forward over the large stile by the gate. By the next gate on the right cross the stile and follow the track into the forest. Ignore minor tracks forking right or left, and at one point a well-made forest road on the right, to keep straight down through the forest. Pass round a gate barring your way, and soon after passing the alternative start (Silton picnic area) the road becomes tarmacked and soon leads out of the forest. Pass Hunter's Hill Farm on the right and Moor House on the left.

When you reach a T junction turn right. Soon the village of Over Silton, our next goal, appears ahead. When you draw level with the church of St Mary, set in the middle of the fields, find a stile by a gate on the right and follow the hedge on your right up to the churchyard, which you enter by a gate beside a mounting block. On leaving the churchyard by the same gate, walk straight across the large field to a stile by the gate at the far end and continue forward on the road through the village. Ignore a public footpath sign pointing right up a track. The road bears right. Before it bears left again leave it up a No Through Road signposted Bridleway to Thimbleby (to the right of Keeper's Cottage on the corner).

Soon after leaving the village take the narrow, steeply ascending path on the left immediately before a Forestry Commission sign (Cleveland Forest: Silton), which leads up to the right of a wall to pass an old gatepost and reach a broad track. Turn left along this and follow it all the way until you emerge from the wood and come to a clear cross-track (leading to a gate a few yards to the left). Turn right up the ascending

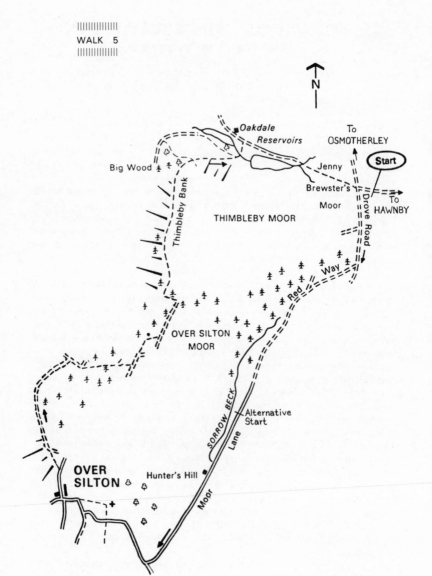

track, but where it bears left keep straight on up a narrow but clear footpath. There are some wet patches where there seem to be several alternative paths, but look forward and you will always see the correct route climbing clearly through the wood. At one point where there is a clear fork keep right on the steeply ascending branch, passing in a few yards a very steep, but masked, drop on the left and soon reaching a cross-track. Turn left along it.

At the next fork keep left along the lower and narrower path, which soon begins to climb steeply, passing a large boulder on the left with a good view of Osmotherley. At the next wide track again turn left, soon to reach a fence at the edge of the forest. Turn left down this fence until you reach a stile in it. Cross this and follow the narrow but clear level path, which can be overgrown, across a delightfully varied stretch of moor, a fine place for bilberries in season. There are extensive views across the Vale of Mowbray to the Pennines.

Eventually you reach a stile in a facing fence and continue forward towards a stand of conifers. Join a cross-track, turn right along it for 5 yards, then leave it by another track on the left, which leads through the trees, through a gap in a wall and over a stile. Now follows another stretch of delightful, level path. Cross another stile in a facing fence and continue forward, now with more mature trees to your left. The next short section can be very overgrown, but press on regardless — the path is never in doubt — soon with a steep wooded slope to your left. Emerge from the woodland onto open moor. At a yellow arrow waymark on a post the path turns sharp left and descends through an area of recently planted trees. Oak Dale and the upper reservoir are visible ahead.

Re-entering more mature woodland the path continues steeply downwards. By another marker post it bears left over a wet and rather smelly area to continue dropping through the trees to a footbridge which can be seen below. Cross the bridge and walk forward to a stile out of the wood. Bear slightly right to the next stile and then forward and again slightly right to join a track. Turn right along it. You are now back on the Cleveland Way. As you walk, look forward and you will see the line of your path climbing the hillside ahead.

Cross a ladder-stile and walk along the left-hand side of the reservoir. At the far end cross the stream by the bridge and begin the steep ascent. As you climb, pause and look back for the view down Oak Dale towards Osmotherley. You reach the road at the car park from which you started.

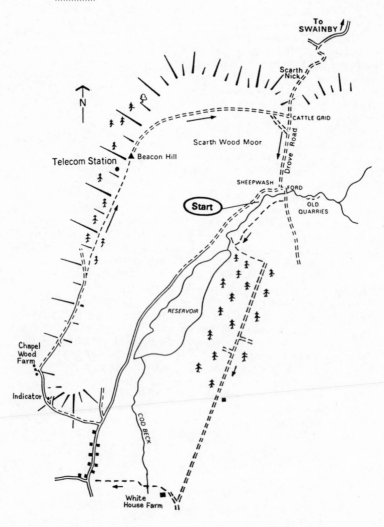

To SWAINBY

Scarth Nick

CATTLE GRID

N

Scarth Wood Moor

Drove Road

Telecom Station ▲ Beacon Hill

SHEEPWASH ⊩ FORD

Start

OLD QUARRIES

RESERVOIR

Chapel Wood Farm

Indicator

COD BECK

White House Farm

OSMOTHERLEY AND
SCARTH WOOD MOOR

WALK 6

★

5 miles (8 km)

On the road northwards out of Osmotherley towards Swainby, nearly 2 miles out of the village and a short distance beyond the reservoir there is a favourite picnic spot by the beck usually known as Sheepwash, with a large gravel car park. Park here (GR 470 994).

Walk upstream to the bridge, cross it and continue uphill on the broad track. After about 50 yards, just before the track becomes more enclosed by rocks on each side, find a narrow path leaving it at right-angles on the right. After a few yards this forks: keep right, and climb steeply up to the edge of the moor. A clear, narrow path contours high above the stream, soon passing the car park far below. Continue along the moor edge, ignoring paths branching left, towards the wood ahead.

Shortly before you reach the trees at a corner of the wood, the path drops slightly to meet a clear cross-path coming up from the stream on the right. Turn left along it, keeping the wood to your right, until you reach a ladder-stile into the wood. Cross it and keep forward on the grassy track, descending slightly to cross a stream, then ascending again to pick up a wall to your right. Keep straight ahead on the track until you meet a forest road, then straight on along this. When the forest road shortly bears right, again keep forward on a track.

Leave the wood by a gate beside a Forestry Commission sign, go through another gate 10 yards further on, and keep on with the wall and wood to your right to pass to the right of a farm and into a hedged lane. Soon Osmotherley with its square church tower comes into view nestling below, with a distant prospect beyond. The track becomes more enclosed and begins to descend. Ten yards before you reach a farm access road, pass through a gap-stile in the hedge on the right with a largely hidden Cleveland Way sign. For most of the rest of the walk you will be on the Cleveland Way.

Join the farm access road and turn right along it. Immediately before the farm (and a large isolated tree) bear right to pass a wooden electricity pole with FOOTPATH painted on it. Pass to the right of the farm to a stile, then straight down the next field to cross a farm track at the bottom and keep forward to cross the stream by a footbridge. Follow the good

23

path up the other side to pass through a stile into a meadow: walk straight across this to a stile by the gate at the far side with the village beyond. Keep forward across the next field to a gap-stile ahead to the left of the wide grass lane (Cleveland Way sign) and continue along the narrow ginnel with a fence to your right.

Emerge through another gap-stile onto a lane, cross slightly right onto a paved, then cobbled, path which leads to the centre of Osmotherley. Turn right along the road to Swainby (the one you motored along earlier) through this lovely village. Having left the houses behind, on the crest of the rise, turn left into Ruebury Lane (Cleveland Way sign). After some time the track forks and it is worth keeping right for a yard or two to find a direction indicator on the left which helps to explain the vast panorama across the Vale of Mowbray.

Continue now on the lower track. The surfacing ends at Chapel Wood Farm, where you keep forward through a kissing-gate (Cleveland Way sign) and on along the grassy track with the hedge to your left. The track enters a wood through a gate and divides. Take the right-hand, ascending branch (Cleveland Way sign). On emerging from the wood again, the track narrows to a clear path, and at the top it meets a facing wall and bears left, never straying far from this wall to reach the British Telecom Microwave Radio Station on Beacon Hill, the site of an ancient signal point. A little further on you will see through a gap in the wall on your right a white triangulation pillar, height 982 ft above sea level, and there are glorious views left.

Follow the wall until two gates give access to Scarth Wood Moor. Ahead of you are three paths: one keeps left, close to the fence on the left, one goes right along the wall on the right and one heads straight across the moor. This is the one to follow. Look right as you walk and you should soon be able to see your car. When your track approaches a wall on the left it forks. Leave the Cleveland Way here and keep right on the higher branch, which soon curves right and descends to join the tarmac road which is the old Drove Road. Turn right and walk along the grassy verge to return to your starting point.

LIVE MOOR, HOLEY MOOR, CARLTON MOOR AND SCUGDALE

WALK 7

★

7 miles (11 km)

I really believe that the best walking country in the National Park is over the 'bumps' of the north-facing hills of the Clevelands, which look so impressive when viewed from the A173 between Great Ayton and Stokesley. Conditions on the well-worn tracks among the heather are ideal for those who like to stride or stroll along the tops. The views of the Cleveland Plain below, with its patchwork of fields of all colours (especially in May, when the oilseed rape is in flower, or at harvest time), the conical shape of Roseberry Topping in the middle distance, and Teesside beyond, all add to the joy of the local scene and the breath of moorland air.

The central feature of these hills is Cringle Moor and today's journey is intended to take in the three moors leading up to a good view of it, as well as a quiet pastoral valley which was once a busy jet-mining area, where although the signs of the mining activities are now very much subdued it is still interesting to observe the lines of the rock strata by the position of the old spoil heaps.

Three miles south-west of Stokesley, just off the main A172, is the very fine village of Carlton-in-Cleveland. Motor up the village street, fork left at the top on the road to Chop Gate and head for the hills. A mile out of the village the road climbs a steep bank, and just over the top is the National Park's Green Bank car park and picnic site (small charge) with the Lord Stones Café, toilets and a telephone. Park here (GR 524 030).

Leave the car park by the path at the opposite end to the entrance and walk forward to a small plantation where there is a plaque in memory of Alec and Annie Falconer 'who loved these hills'. Pass to the left of it and at the Cleveland Way signpost turn left on a green track across the moor to reach the motor road over a stile by a gate and another Cleveland Way sign. Go right along the road for a few yards before turning left at the next Cleveland Way sign through a gate and along a track, which is in fact the access road to the Newcastle and Teesside Gliding Club. The old alum mine workings which abound here are dangerous and should not be explored.

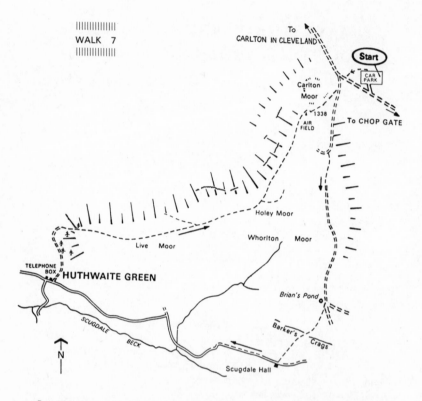

To
CARLTON IN CLEVELAND

Start

CAR
PARK

Carlton
Moor

1338

AIR
FIELD

To CHOP GATE

Holey Moor

Whorlton   Moor

Live   Moor

TELEPHONE
BOX
HUTHWAITE GREEN

Brian's Pond

SCUGDALE   BECK

Barker's   Crags

N

Scugdale Hall

In 100 yards the Cleveland Way leaves the track and ascends the hillside on the right (our return route) but we keep to the track (signposted Bridleway). Ignore a forestry road forking off left and stay on the ascending track, which offers fine views down Bilsdale. Just after an old quarry on the right and opposite the last of the telegraph poles on the left, the track bears right but we keep forward on a grassy path through the heather, the start of which is marked by two small cairns. Soon the buildings of the Gliding Club are visible to your right, and on breasting the rise you come to an open space free of heather with a broad track a few yards to your right. Join this and turn left along it in the direction of the television mast in the distance.

The track soon bears sharply right, passes to the right of a scattering of rocks surmounted by a cairn and joins another clear track coming from the gliding field: turn left along this, still in the direction of the TV mast. Immediately after passing to the left of Brian's Pond in the dip and 30 yards before the track forks, turn right at a bridleway sign along a track which is much less distinct. In 150 yards bear slightly right off this track on a narrow but clear path to pass immediately to the left of another pond. The clear path, which at times may be obscured by deep heather, leads forward to the edge of the moor, from where you look down into Scugdale, and begins to descend.

Ignore paths left and right and descend to pass through a wide gap in a wall and 5 yards beyond it a bridle-gate. The rocky escarpment is to your right. From the gate the path is still clear as it descends past a bridleway sign, then becomes less distinct as it passes over some rather wet ground with many rushes. Make your way, as dryshod as you can, to the right-hand end of the facing wall, pass it and continue down, with a stream to your right, to a facing gate. Through this, follow the wall/fence to your right down to join the road through Scugdale by another gate at Scugdale Hall.

Turn right along the road, tarmacked from this point, and follow it down lovely Scugdale until you reach the crossroads by the telephone kiosk at Huthwaite Green. Here you rejoin the Cleveland Way. Turn right through the gate and along the good track. After passing old iron mine workings on the left the track bears right and a ladder-stile gives access to a steep stepped path up through the forest. Near the top, cross over a track and continue forward to cross a step-stile onto the open moor. The clear path continues to ascend across Live Moor.

The view is superb over the Cleveland Plain. Immediately to your left is the wooded outlier of Whorl Hill with the hamlet of Faceby to the right of it; further off is Middlesbrough, with Roseberry Topping to the right of it. After passing the cairn on the top of Live Moor the ground dips a little and gently rises onto Holey Moor. On Carlton Moor you reach the broad swathe bulldozed for the use of the Gliding Club: our route first lies along the left-hand edge of this, then diverges left to keep closer to the edge of the escarpment.

When you are opposite the buildings of the Gliding Club you can either keep on the main track straight ahead or follow a narrower path closer to the edge. Both lead to the trig point above Carlton Bank, at 1,338 ft the climax of today's walk and a viewpoint to be savoured. The clear track now turns due south and soon descends through extensive mine workings (please keep to the waymarked path) to rejoin the track used at the start of the walk. Retrace your outward route to return to the car.

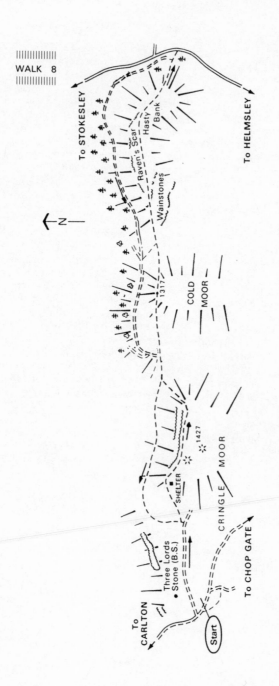

←N—

To STOKESLEY

To HELMSLEY

Raven's Scar

Hasty Bank

Wainstones

1317

COLD MOOR

1427

CRINGLE MOOR

SHELTER

Three Lords Stone (B.S.)

To CARLTON

To CHOP GATE

Start

CRINGLE MOOR, COLD MOOR AND HASTY BANK

WALK 8

★

7 miles (11 km)

This is the most spectacular walk in the book, but also the most strenuous, involving three steep ascents and three steep descents, sometimes on badly eroded paths. Having done it, you will also have got to know one of the most impressive sections of both the Cleveland Way and the Coast to Coast Walk.

The starting point is the same as for Walk 7, the National Park's Green Bank car park and picnic site at the top of Carlton Bank (GR 524 030).

Leave the car park by the path at the opposite end to the entrance, but having passed the small plantation, turn right by the Cleveland Way sign and follow the clear grassy track. A slight diversion here towards the edge of the moor would bring you to the big square rock known as the Three Lords Stone, the meeting point of three old estates.

Your route can be seen ascending the hillside ahead on the right-hand side of a wall. At the top a substantial wind shelter has been built (for about three people) in front of which there is a direction indicator dedicated to Alec Falconer. Just after this, your return path can clearly be seen below on the left. The views are superb. Looking south, the highest point of Cringle Moor (1,427 ft) is about ¼ of a mile from the edge, but it is not much higher than your present path and there is little to be gained by going inland.

Your track keeps close to the moor edge above some crags and soon begins to descend steeply towards Cold Moor, the next top to attack. Drop down to the dip, past some slag heaps on the left, cross a stream in a wet patch of ground, and on reaching two upright stones, previously used as gateposts, bear to the right. Pass through a gate and climb steeply to the top of Cold Moor, to its highest point on the northern edge at 1,317 ft. As on Cringle, the path on Cold Moor keeps nearly to the left-hand edge, and ahead will soon be seen the crags of the Wainstones on Hasty Bank. The steep path will take you down and up to them, and although they may look like an impregnable barrier from a distance, the clear path winds its way up through them without the slightest difficulty. There may be rock climbers at work, because the climbs include clefts, faces and even a needle.

The tendency so far will have been for the eye to wander to the left over the Cleveland Plain but at the Wainstones there is a good view to the right. Bilsdale is to the south, and to the south-east is Urra Moor where there is the highest point on the North York Moors, marked by a trig point at 1,489 ft.

To complete the outward journey go over the top of Hasty Bank and steeply down towards the Bilsdale road, the main road from Stokesley to Helmsley. Cross a stile by a memorial bench into forestry land, but instead of bearing right with the Cleveland Way down to the road, turn left up the broad track between the fence on the left and the forest on the right. (Incidentally, if you did go down to the road and turned left for a short distance along it, you would come to the Forestry Commission's Clay Bank car park, which would make an alternative starting point for the walk.)

Your clear track curls round the end of Hasty Bank, the cliffs of Raven's Scar are in front of you and Broughton Plantation below to your right. The views across the plain are still excellent, and your almost level track (an old jet miners' path) makes for very pleasant walking. Eventually you cross a stile and a stream and return to the two old gateposts encountered earlier. Avoid the grassy path descending right and keep forward on your outward route. Cross the stream and the boggy patch but a few yards further on instead of ascending steeply the way you came down, fork right on a clear contouring path which passes to the left of a spoil heap.

There are many remains of industrial activity on the next section, but your route is never in doubt, and eventually the contouring path leads you back to rejoin your outward route once more, not far away from the car park.

TRIPSDALE, URRA MOOR
AND BOTTON HEAD

WALK 9

★

5 or 10½ miles (8 or 17 km)

A delightful hidden valley, a prehistoric earthwork, a leg-stretching moor-land tramp to the highest point on the North York Moors, Botton Head at 1,489 ft, some old guideposts and boundary stones and glorious views: these are some of the pleasures of today's ramble.

The starting point is the free car park (with toilets) just south of Chop Gate on the B1257 Helmsley to Stokesley road (GR 558 994).

Leave the car park and turn right along the road as far as the access road to Esp House on the left. Three yards after this drive, cross the fence on the left and bear half-right across the large field to a stile in the top right-hand corner. Turn left up the access road to William Beck Farm. The track bears right across the front of the farmhouse to a gate, soon bearing right between walls to another gate. Through this fork left up a walled lane.

Where the lane ends pass through a gate and keep forward on the track to another gate in the opposite wall. A clear path continues forward uphill through the bracken. Pass through another gate and keep forward to a clear cross-track. Turn right, but very soon at another crossing (there is a standing stone a few yards to the right) turn left again. You may be able to see the clear line of the old track to Bransdale ascending the hill in the distance. The valley in front of you is Tripsdale. The path heads straight for the valley. Shortly before you reach the bottom, you come to a clear cross-path. The walk will continue left here, but before that turn right and go down to the ford, a lovely green spot which tempts one to linger.

Now retrace your steps uphill, keeping straight forward. Pass a small cairn and continue on parallel to the valley down to your right. At another cairn you reach a T junction: turn right, still on a clear path, but after 100 yards fork left on another clear path, which soon turns sharp left and ascends by a line of shooting butts and standing stones, becoming a clear track. At butt 9 you are joined by a clear track from the left. Keep forward, with a wall close by on your left. Chop Gate can be seen ahead in the valley. Soon your track bears right away from the wall, following the line of the old earthworks. Pass a conifer plantation down on the left and some time later you reach a T junction where there is a Nawton

31

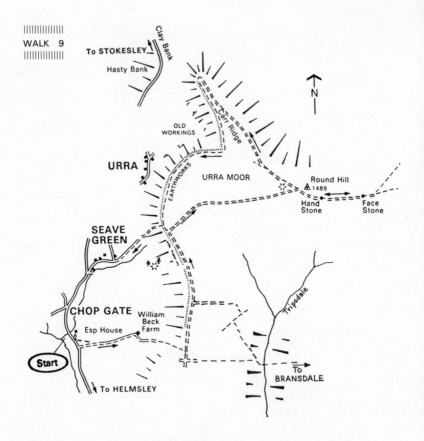

Tower Estate notice and a sign pointing right to Bloworth Crossing.

The SHORTER WALK turns left here downhill (for the rest of the description turn to the last paragraph). For the MAIN WALK turn right and enjoy a glorious moorland tramp, with distant views both north to Cringle Moor, Hasty Bank, Middlesbrough, Roseberry Topping and the Captain Cook Monument and south down Bilsdale. One and a half miles on this wide track brings you to a conical cairn on the left and 50 yards further on to a junction with a similar track coming in from the left: here you join the Cleveland Way. It is often misty here, when the cairn between the routes cannot be seen, but the identity of the junction can be confirmed by observing a short standing boundary stone on the north side of the track carved with the initials AM.

Turn right along the track, in 100 yards looking out for a clear narrow path left to the triangulation pillar on the tumulus of Round Hill, the highest point in the National Park, but a rather disappointing viewpoint. To return to the track take another path slightly left of the one you came by, and you will reach another boundary stone. This is the Hand Stone; a hand carved on the south face points to the east and says 'This is the way to KIR' (Kirkbymoorside) and on the other side the hand faces west with the words 'This is the way to STO' (Stokesley). About 300 yards further along the track is the Face Stone on which, facing east, is carved a face, and on the top KIR.

Now retrace your steps to the junction, this time taking the right fork. Follow the clear track until, shortly after a wall comes to within 20 yards of the track on the right, you reach a gate and the ground falls steeply ahead. Thirty yards before the gate take a clear path forking sharply back on the left with a wall about 20 yards away on the right. You have now rejoined the line of the old earthwork. There is one cross-path to be ignored before you cross a deep ravine with the infant Bilsdale Beck. The clear path continues on the other side. Shortly you will notice what seems to be a large rock 50 yards to the right of the path. It is in fact an outcrop, and it is worth making the short detour to it for good views of the scene below: some signs of old workings all along at a lower level, the farms of the hamlet of Urra, and a profile of the Wainstones at the far end of Hasty Bank on the opposite side of Bilsdale, and comprehensive views of the top end of this lovely valley.

Return to your path and continue along it. There is one more minor ravine to be crossed and then, about 100 yards before you reach a wall coming up from the right, there is a boggy patch where you might lose the path. Keep straight forward to the wall, because the path continues along the left-hand side of it. Some distance after the wall ends you reach a cross-track and turn right down it. You are now back on the route of the shorter walk.

[Walkers on the SHORTER WALK resume here.] The track drops to a stile by a gate and continues downhill, passing to the left of an old stone building. Pass through a gateway in a wall and keep on down with a wall to your right. Cross a stile by a gate and continue along the track, soon with a steep drop to your left. Pass through two gates at Bilsdale Hall and turn left down the road through Seave Green. A few yards after crossing the bridge over Bilsdale Beck you reach the main road, where you turn left to walk through Chop Gate and return to the car.

COW RIDGE, HEAD HOUSE AND ARNSGILL RIDGE

WALK 10

★

5½ miles (8.5 km)

This is a walk on good tracks through lovely heather country, at its best in late August, up one side of the valley of Arns Gill and down the other. A great opportunity to step out, to take in great gulps of pure air and to admire the stretches of moorland, ridge upon ridge.

Going towards Osmotherley from Hawnby, first pass Moor Gate, the starting point of Walk 13; a mile further on there is a fine viewpoint at Ellers Wood which is worth a stop. Then the road goes downhill through woods, over Blow Gill — a pretty spot where there is a footbridge — rises from it for half a mile, then makes a long descent to a bridge over the infant river Rye. The road makes a sharp right-hand bend and begins to climb again. Just after the bridge is a large layby on the left often used in the summer as a picnic place. Park here (GR 511 944). Coming from Osmotherley, look out for the sharp left-hand bend and bridge at the foot of a long steep descent, and park on the right.

Walk over the bridge and up the road in the direction of Hawnby. Just past the first farm on the right (Plane Tree Farm) notice an old limekiln on the left; there is a lovely view right to Hawnby Hill and Easterside Hill.

Where the road makes a sharp turn right and starts to descend, take the farm access road on the left over a cattle grid (private road to Scotland Farm). Where this road bends right down to the farm, keep straight ahead along a track through a gate. Climb steadily up Cow Ridge, and when you reach a slender cairn a view of the head of the valley on the left, Arns Gill, opens up, with Head House.

Continue on the ridge track, ignoring first a track forking left, then another forking right, before your track bears left and starts to descend. A track comes in from the right and your track again bears left, down to the valley. It crosses a cattle grid, descends to cross the beck and rises to Head House, a disused farmhouse which is kept in good repair and commands a very fine view down the valley.

At the house the track bears sharp left and rises to cross a cattle grid. When you are joined by another clear track coming from the right you have the opportunity to extend the walk by turning right along it for a

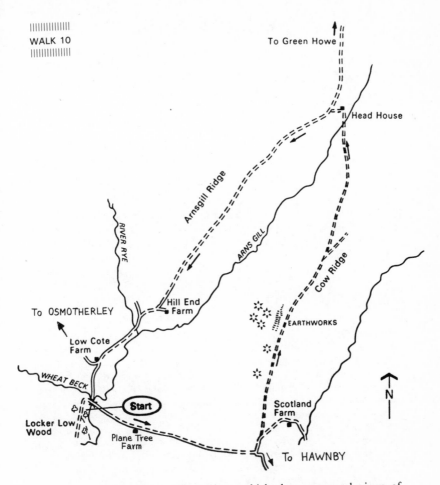

To Green Howe

Head House

Arnsgill Ridge

RIVER RYE

ARNS GILL

Cow Ridge

Hill End Farm

To OSMOTHERLEY

Low Cote Farm

EARTHWORKS

WHEAT BECK

Locker Low Wood

Start

Plane Tree Farm

Scotland Farm

N

To HAWNBY

mile to a tumulus, Green Howe, from which there are good views of Scugdale and Raisdale, then returning by the same route to this point. But the main walk keeps forward.

After passing through a gate, it has a wall to the left; after another gate the wall is to the right — in a few yards keep right at the fork, down the wallside. Pass to the right of a barn and keep forward to a gate into the farmyard at Hill End Farm. After a few yards bear right along the farm access road. At a T junction with another farm road go left. Cross the river Rye by a footbridge at a water splash and continue to Low Cote Farm where you join the Osmotherley to Hawnby road. Continue downhill to return to the car.

NEWGATE BANK

WALK 11

★

4 miles (6.5 km)

Drive north on the Helmsley to Stokesley road as far as the well-signposted Forestry Commission Newgate Bank picnic place on the right, which contains extensive parking facilities and toilets (GR 564 890).
   As you drive in you pass a signpost saying Footpath to Cowhouse Bank, and where after a few yards the track to the picnic site bears left, the right of way goes over the stile by the wide gate ahead. That is the route of our walk, but first drive through the picnic site until you reach a signpost pointing left to 'Viewpoint': park near here and walk down to the stone belvedere for a magnificent view of Bilsdale to the north and the tabular hills above Hawnby to the north-west. The nearer one is Easterside Hill. The views are so extensive on this walk that it is worth taking a smaller scale map with you to fill in the details.

Now EITHER return on foot to the gate near the entrance to the picnic site, cross the stile and follow the forest road, eventually passing through a gateway where the trees on the right are replaced by heather moorland but the good forest road continues, OR, for an alternative start on pleasanter paths with better views, when you leave the belvedere, instead of returning to the car park, take the path dropping sharply left to a track below and turn right along this. When the track ends at a hurdle out of the forest (it is at present blocked by a fallen tree at this point), a narrower path continues just inside the forest boundary fence, giving glorious views. Soon the path bears right away from the edge, passes through an old gateway and joins the forest road and the right of way by which the route of the main walk has come.
   Turn left along the forest road and follow it all the way to where, some distance after passing a trig point, you are faced by a wooden step-stile giving access to a motor road coming up from Helmsley down to your right. All along this stretch there are far-reaching views both to left and to right. By the road there is a bench and you will also see the remains of a sculpture by Austin Wright, erected amidst some controversy in 1977. A public footpath continues ahead along the edge to Cowhouse Bank, but today we turn left along the road, which drops down Helmsley Bank.
   The macadam ends at the foot of the hill at a junction of tracks. Turn left (public footpath sign) and follow this forest road, which also affords pleasant views, ignoring all minor tracks branching off it, all the way back

36

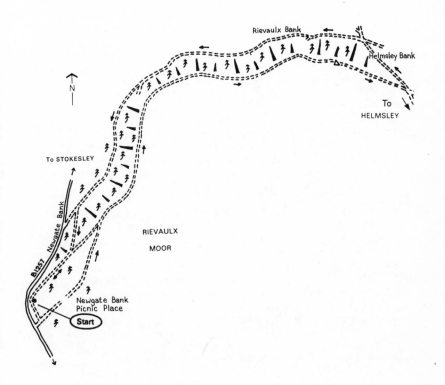

to within 200 yards of the main Helmsley to Stokesley road you started out from. At this point a hurdle gives access to a steeply ascending track on the left, which leads back up to the hurdle by the fallen tree encountered on the alternative start to the walk. Turn right along the track, and on reaching the viewing platform bear left up to the car park.

ROUND EASTERSIDE HILL

WALK 12

★

4½ miles (7 km)

The view from the top of Easterside Hill must be one of the best in the district, but as there is no access to the summit we must content ourselves with walking round it, using a farm track, a moorland way through heather, and a minor road. Because of the stretch over the moor this walk is not recommended in poor visibility.

Motoring north from Helmsley on the road to Stokesley, 1½ miles after passing the picnic site at Newgate Bank Top, a minor road forks left signposted to Laskill. Follow it over the bridge (river Seph) at Laskill, and at the bend shortly afterwards keep straight on ('No Through Road' sign) to park 70 yards further on where there is room at another hairpin bend for more than a dozen cars (GR 562 912).

Walk on along this road. After passing two farms the road turns uphill and before the top is reached take the track on the left signposted to Ewe Cote. When you reach the farm bear slightly right through the yard and pass through a gate leading into a walled lane, which goes uphill and soon leads to another gate into open fields. Continue up with a broken wall to your left, to a stile by a gate in the top corner of the field leading out onto the open moor.

Although the moorland section is quite short, attention must be paid to route-finding. Walk straight forward on the track which leads into a gulley, but very soon the gulley divides and a clear but narrow path heads up between the two branches. After about 200 yards you reach a cross-path which looks as though it might be a cart-track but isn't: turn left along it, and in a few yards it bears slightly right. If you pause here to admire the scene you will notice that Easterside on your left has a very steep northern aspect; in front of you is Hawnby Hill, an isolated tabular similar in many ways to Easterside; to the right in the north can be seen the television mast on Bilsdale West Moor.

Ahead is a wall, and the clear path leads you to what looks like a gap but is in fact a gate, well to the right of Easterside Hill. Pass through the gate and keep forward to follow the fence on your right. About 200 yards before High Banniscue Farm, go through a gate in the fence and turn left along the track to the farm. Just before the farm cross the stile by the gate and immediately bear left (public bridleway sign) on the track which leads

38

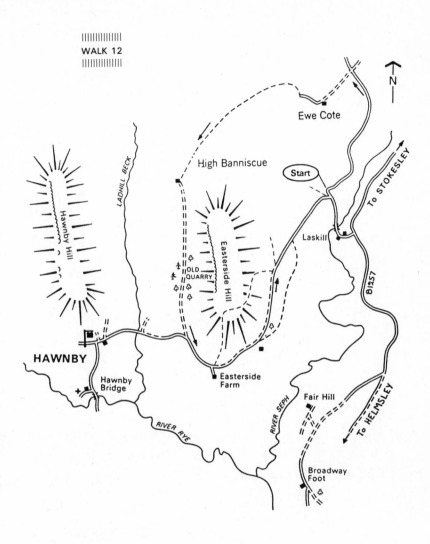

Ewe Cote

High Banniscue

Start

To STOKESLEY

LADHILL BECK

Hawnby Hill

Easterside Hill

OLD QUARRY

Laskill

B1257

HAWNBY

Hawnby
Bridge

Easterside
Farm

RIVER SEPH

Fair Hill

To HELMSLEY

RIVER RYE

Broadway
Foot

round above all the farm buildings, to join the farm access road by a telegraph pole. Keep ahead down the road.

Just before you meet the next motor road, look right for an attractive view of the village of Hawnby nestling among the hills. Turn left on the road and follow it all the way back to the bend with the no through road sign to the left. The car is 70 yards along this.

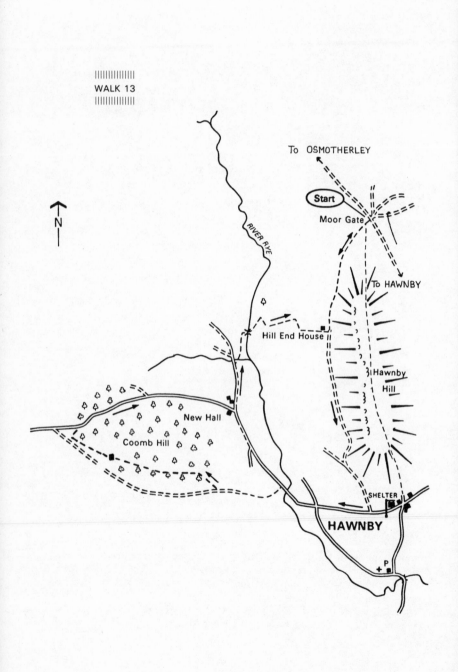

WALK 13

To OSMOTHERLEY

Start

Moor Gate

RIVER RYE

To HAWNBY

Hill End House

Hawnby Hill

New Hall

Coomb Hill

SHELTER

HAWNBY

N

P

ALONGSIDE HAWNBY HILL AND AROUND COOMB HILL

WALK 13

★

5 miles (8 km)

It is unfortunate that because there is no right of way over the top of the central feature in the Hawnby area the reader cannot be guided along this fine hog's back which provides an exhilarating mile of ridge walking. But there are lovely places which can be visited, as this walk will show.

Motoring north from Hawnby on the Osmotherley road you cross a cattle grid to reach an open space where several tracks meet. This is Moor Gate. Park here (GR 539 917).

Walk back over the cattle grid and immediately turn right (public bridleway sign) onto a clear track, but after a few yards fork left off it again onto a fainter, grassy track which crosses a third track and then heads gently up round the end of Hawnby Hill (don't be tempted to take the track further left which leads up the ridge of the hill itself). With glorious views over upper Ryedale on the right, the track soon drops gently towards a fence and joins a clearer track coming down from the hill. Follow the fence down to Hill End House, pass to the left of this and keep on the clear track all the way down to a motor road.

Unless refreshment is required at the Hawnby Hotel, a short distance to the left, turn right down the road. Beyond the crossroads where there is a notice saying 'Unsuitable for Motors 1½ miles ahead', cross Church Bridge over the river Rye and immediately turn sharp left along a track (public bridleway sign). Pass through a gate and follow the track for 30 yards beside the river before forking right uphill towards a tree and then a power line pole. Cross a stile by a gate and continue on the grassy track, passing through another gate, which says 'Beware of the Bull', then forking right on the ascending track.

Don't go through the gate ahead in the top corner, marked private, but just before it turn sharp left and follow the track to another gate into the woods. After some time keep right at a fork. On leaving the wood through a gate at a ruined building bear half-left down the large field to a gate leading back into the woodland ahead (note that it is *not* the gate you can see in the valley bottom, but one at present invisible further to the right of it — it has a blue waymark on it). The track leads down to the right of a ravine; passage is impeded at the moment by fallen trees, but a way can be found round to the right of them. The track leads to a motor road by a public bridleway sign.

Turn right down the road. Ahead can be seen the cliffs of Hawnby Hill, and the farm below the cliffs is Hill End House, which we shall pass again later. When, at New Hall, the first buildings by the roadside are arrived at, turn left through the gate to pass between buildings onto a track, passing a cottage on the left. The track leads down to a stream over which there is a stout plank bridge, but instead of crossing this go through the gateway on the right leading to a path across the corner of the field to a wooden footbridge. Walk down the left bank of the stream, bearing left to a gate, after which the track continues with the young river Rye down on the right, soon to be crossed by a metal footbridge, a delightful spot.

Turn to the left on the other side and follow the clear path as it winds up the hillside to a gate in the corner of a field. Go through this and turn right up the edge of the field to reach another gate in it near the top right-hand corner of the field. Pass through this and walk forward on the grassy track; at the top of the rise bear left, passing a line of trees, to reach Hill End House. Make for the gate on the right of the house, which gives access to the track used earlier. Turn left and retrace your steps, remembering to keep straight ahead in the direction of the television mast (Bilsdale) when the clearer track bears right up the hillside.

THORODALE

WALK 14

★

7 miles (11 km)

The lovely little village of Hawnby, situated on a hillside and surrounded by tabular hills of notable shape, can easily be reached by car from Helmsley by taking the Stokesley road and forking left after about 3 miles. It can also be reached from Thirsk via Boltby and Sneck Yate Bank or from Osmotherley on the narrow road via Snilesworth, all three routes presenting most beautiful scenery.

The walk passes through wooded country and into the secluded bracken-covered valley of Thorodale, then crosses a section of heather moorland to reach the famous Hambleton Drove Road for a glimpse of the Vale of Mowbray and, with luck, of the Pennines beyond. It returns along a road unsuitable for motors, giving lovely views of the lake in the valley below and the tabular hills.

Take the Kepwick road out of Hawnby, passing a sign saying 'Unsuitable for Motors 1½ miles ahead' and cross the fine stone Church Bridge over the river Rye. The road makes a sharp left-hand turn at New Hall and 100 yards further on there is room to park in a layby on the left (GR 530 905), but please do not obstruct the gate (if this is full, there is another layby on the left less than ½ a mile further on, shortly after passing a farm access road which forks right).

In either case walk back down the road to New Hall and turn left along the track between the buildings. It leads downhill between trees to a stream which you cross by a sleeper bridge, then uphill again. When the track forks, keep right and continue up to a gate out of the woodland. Follow the edge of the field with the wood to your right, cross a stile onto a farm access road and turn left along it. Walk straight through the farmyard at Mount Pleasant to the far end and bear left over a cattle-grid, still on a good track. After 200 yards go through the gate to the right of a clump of trees (a notice on it says 'Beware of Bull') and walk along the edge of the field with the hedge to your left. At the end of the field keep forward through the gateway and continue with the fence to your left.

Soon a rear view of Arden Hall is seen on the left. Pass through the gate at the end of the field. A good track comes up from the left, from Arden Hall, but your way lies straight ahead, taking the left-hand fork of the two tracks to your right, uphill, with trees to your left. Where the ground levels out keep right at the fork on the better of the two tracks,

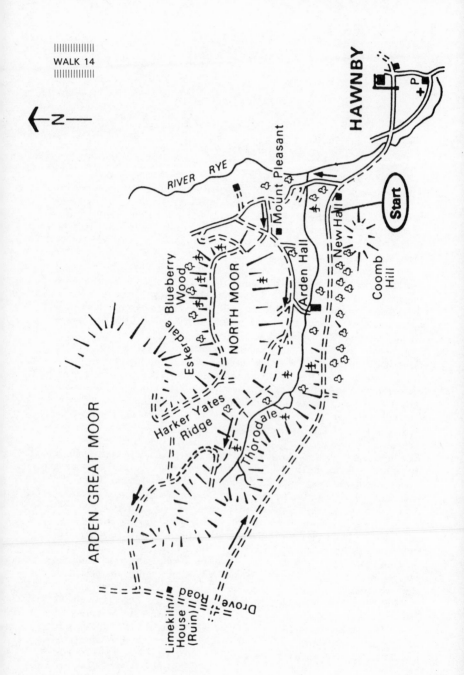

N

HAWNBY

RIVER RYE

Mount Pleasant

Blueberry Wood

Eskerdale

NORTH MOOR

Arden Hall

New Hall

Coomb Hill

Start

P

Harker Yates Ridge

Thirodale

ARDEN GREAT MOOR

Limekiln House (Ruin)

Drove Road

which soon begins to ascend again. Pheasant rearing is much in evidence around here. Ignore minor tracks branching left and right ('Private' notices will sometimes help to keep you on the right way). At a major crossing of tracks keep straight ahead, and at the next fork keep right.

Eventually the track leads out of the wood at a gate. A few yards further on turn sharp right at the T junction on a grassy track slanting back up the hillside. There are fine views of Thorodale, including the lake. Towards the top the track bears left across heather moorland. You are joined by another good track from the right. There now follows an easy, level tramp on a good track through the heather. When you reach a grassy area with a marker post numbered 5 on the left, keep straight ahead up the good track. You reach the Drove Road at a facing wall. Turn left along it. By a gateway you pass the few remains of Lime Kiln House, years ago a public house serving chiefly the drovers who used this ancient way to bring their cattle from Scotland to the markets of the south, mainly York and Malton. The herds would be driven through Yarm and onto the high ground of the North York Moors at Scarth Nick near Swainby, over Black Hambleton and south past where we are now standing to the Hambleton Hotel and beyond. Nowadays the road is used a great deal by walkers and part of it has been incorporated into the Cleveland Way and the White Rose Walk.

On a clear day the view from here is superb. It is pretty below around the villages of Kepwick and the Siltons, Nether and Over, and the extensive views over the Vale of Mowbray include Wensleydale, with Penhill on its southern edge and, south of that, Great Whernside above the general line of the Pennines.

When the tarmacked road from Kepwick comes up from the right through a white gate, fork left off the Drove Road on a stony track. This track, which becomes tarmacked at Arden Hall, leads all the way back to the car. There are lovely views of the tabular hills on the way down. At one point you are joined by another track snaking down from the right (look over the wall on the left just after this point for a fine view of Thorodale and the lake). As you pass the drive to Arden Hall look left for a glimpse of this beautiful Queen Anne stone house, built on the site of a medieval nunnery.

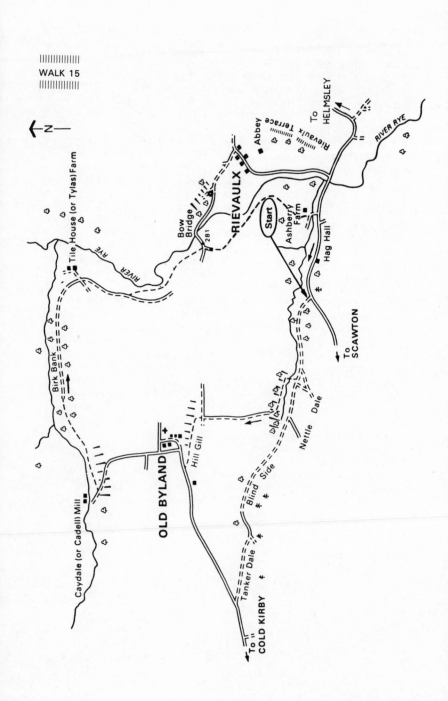

||||||||||||||
WALK 15
||||||||||||||

←N—

RIEVAULX AND RYEDALE

WALK 15

★

6 miles (9.5 km)

No visitor to the National Park should fail to visit Rievaulx Abbey, one of the finest Cistercian ruins in England. The abbey was founded in 1131, but not completed until the mid-13th century. The setting in the Rye valley (Rievaulx is Rye vallis) is perfect: the surrounding hills and trees add beauty to the scene and the little village of Rievaulx is itself worth a visit. The 18th century Rievaulx Terrace, above the abbey, should not be missed either, with its ½ mile of lawn, two classical temples and some of the best views of the abbey. Our walk today will give views of the abbey and the terrace from the other side of the river and includes a section of the Cleveland Way and some very fine valley and woodland scenery.

To reach the starting point by car from Helmsley, take the Stokesley road and after little more than a mile turn left on the road signposted to Scawton and Old Byland. On reaching the valley look right for a view of the abbey, but go forward over Rievaulx Bridge. Continue towards Scawton for ¾ mile, ignoring a minor road on the right which crosses a small brick bridge, and just after the road bends left there is room to park the car beside a track on the right leading up to a gate into woodland (GR 563 845).

Go through the gate, on which is the acorn sign of the Cleveland Way, and through the woods on a track above the stream and a succession of three ponds on the right. Leave the track when it bears left and cross a footbridge over the clear limestone stream, in which watercress grows, to a wicket gate and a path through the thicket. Take only 15 paces on this path and, leaving the Cleveland Way, turn right to a stile into the water meadow. Cross this to another footbridge and take the path to the left sloping up the hill through the woods. At the top pass through a bridle-gate into a field and continue forward through this field and the next one with the hedge to your right, to a gate by a power line pole. Walk forward, crossing a track, to the next gate directly ahead. Old Byland village is in front of you.

Turn left along a path high above the wooded ravine of Hill Gill, which soon rises to meet you, so that the path crosses it without noticeably losing height and then rises to a gate and the road just outside the village, close to the County Council millstone village sign. Turn right, and either turn left along the road just before the centre of the village or else join this

47

road by going through the village, turning left at the top end and right at the next junction.

Shortly after leaving the village the main road turns left, but you keep straight ahead along a road signposted as 'Unsuitable for Motor Vehicles'. The road takes you northwards towards Caydale (or Cadell) Mill. Where it turns left at the top of the hill, stop to admire the valley view. Go down the road almost to the bottom of the hill and through a gate on the right (bridleway sign), keeping forward across the field to pick up a broken wall, which you keep on your left, to a gate into the wood. The path through the wood along Birk Bank is clear, and you reach a metalled road above Tylas Farm.

Keep straight forward along it, and after ½ mile at a dip in the road go over a stile by a gate on the left. The path is clear through the field, a section on the steep river bank is board-walked, then there is another stile to be crossed before the path leads you to a lane by a footpath sign pointing back to Hawnby. Turn right for a few yards, then left through a gate signposted to Ashberry, on a track which is unmistakable, first below the woods then through them round Ashberry Hill. When eventually another track comes in from the right, keep forward for glorious views to the abbey and the Ionic temple on the terrace above. On emerging by Ashberry Farm walk forward to the road, turn left over the bridge and then right along the road (and Cleveland Way) to return to the car.

DALE TOWN AND RYEDALE

WALK 16

★

7 miles (11 km)

From Thirsk, drive to Boltby and continue up the steep Sneck Yate Bank, then follow the signpost for Hawnby 2½. Shortly after coming to the end of a wood on the left, the view opens out and soon you pass the end of a minor road on the right. A little further, just before the 25% gradient sign, there is a public bridleway sign on the left (pointing up a track through a gate on the right) and a layby on the right. Park here.

Coming from Helmsley, take the Stokesley road and turn left when a minor road on the left is signposted to Hawnby. At the T junction, where Hawnby is a short distance to the right, turn left and ascend the steep Murton Bank. The layby is at the end of the wood on the left (GR 537 884).

Walk along the road in the direction of Boltby, and opposite the minor road on the left go through the gate on the right (bridleway sign) and walk down the track (glorious views). About 100 yards before a gate across the track, a bridleway sign shows the direction of the path to Dale Town: it forks right off the track, then sharply right downhill towards a cross-hedge coming up from the farm. Soon join a rather wider grassy track and follow it to the right of an ash tree, then bear left down the field, parallel to the hedge on your left, to Dale Town Farm. A few yards before reaching the buildings bear right to cross a cattle-grid, then pass straight through the farmyard to a gate. Walk straight on with a fence to your left to another gate.

The track now forks: bear left on the higher branch. You walk parallel to a stream down on your right to a gate in the fence ahead. Continue forward to pass to the left of the abandoned Gowerdale House. In front of it a bridleway sign (to Noddle End) points left up the hill: follow this, passing to the right of a large ash tree, then bearing right up to a gate in the wall ahead. An old sign on the gate bids one beware of the bull. A few yards further on, cross straight over a good track and continue steeply uphill on a narrow path. In a few more yards you meet another cross-track: turn left up it, soon bearing right with it up by the side of a wood. Shortly it bears slightly right away from the wood (there is a good view back) to pass to the right of a ruined building. Turn uphill again along the side of this ruin, before bearing right and slanting up to the brow of the hill.

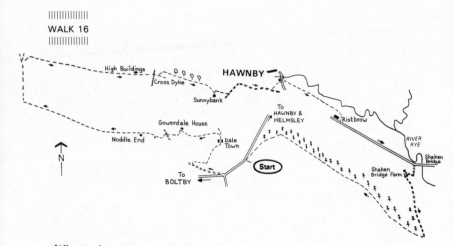

When a barn up to your left comes in sight, bear left to walk straight uphill and pass to the right of the barn: the gap in the wall has been blocked, but the wall can be easily climbed. Now continue forward with a wall to your left. Pass through a gate and keep straight on: you may pass through fields of oats, barley and potatoes. Shortly after passing a small wooden and corrugated iron shed you come to a second gate across the track at the end of the cultivated fields. Pass through the gate and turn right along the green way with the wall to your right.

The track bears slightly left away from the wall. After a slight dip, which is in fact the head of Gower Dale which you can see on your right, the track divides into several branches: bear slightly right, still on a good grassy track, soon to pick up a fence to your right which you follow to a gate in the wall ahead. Pass through and keep forward with a wall/fence to your left. Now you are back in cultivated fields. Pass to the right of the barns called High Buildings on the map and keep on down the track. Having passed through a gap in the next facing wall, built on the line of an earthwork called Cross Dyke, the track forks. Keep left to descend beside a wood.

A few yards before Sunnybank Farm the track again forks: keep left, and then shortly before the buildings themselves turn left down another track. In a very short distance bear right off it to pass through a gate and walk down the edge of the field with the hedge to your left to join the farm access track through a white gate. Turn left down the track. At the foot of the hill cross the stream by the cattle-grid bridge and in a few yards cross the stile in the fence on the left. Bear very slightly right across the next field to another stile in the far left-hand corner. Turn left along the road. Just before the bridge cross a stile in the fence on the right. Bear slightly right up the bank and walk straight across the field to a hurdle in the fence ahead, just to the left of a solitary hawthorn tree. Bear very slightly right across the next field to a gate in the fence ahead and keep forward, eventually picking up a track which leads up to Ristbrow Farm on the right. At the far end of the buildings pass through a gate and walk forward, then bear left to another gate and the road.

Turn left along the road. There are pleasant views of Ryedale. Descend an 11% gradient and at the foot, shortly before the road crosses the Rye by Shaken Bridge, turn right up the access road to Shaken Bridge Farm. The road bends sharp right, then at the farm bear sharp left through the yard, round the back of the farmhouse on the left, and on up the broad track. A few yards after passing the corner of a wood on the right the track forks: keep right. There is a fine view back. When you reach the top edge of the wood on your right the track swings sharp right through a gate. Follow it along the top side of the wood, passing a barn. Ignore the first gate into the wood, but go through the second.

The track, which for much of its length is just a path, is never far from the top edge of the wood. It is obstructed by a goodly number of fallen trees, all easily negotiable. You will only come to one fork, where you must keep left close to the top edge of the wood. Eventually the path joins a better track by a bridleway sign beside a gate. Keep left, soon passing to the side of a gate and returning to the car.

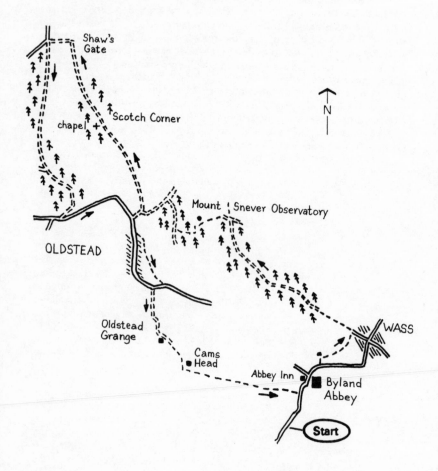

Shaw's
Gate

Scotch Corner

chapel +

N

Mount Snever Observatory

OLDSTEAD

WASS

Oldstead
Grange

Cams
Head

Abbey Inn

Byland
Abbey

Start

BYLAND ABBEY,
MOUNT SNEVER OBSERVATORY
AND SCOTCH CORNER

WALK 17

★

5 or 8 miles (8 or 13 km)

This walk through lovely wooded countryside visits a ruined Cistercian abbey, a Victorian observatory, a modern chapel with fine stone and wood carvings and the site of a medieval battle, and traverses two old roads with excellent views.

The starting point is a loop of old road forming a layby 300 yards south of Byland Abbey on the road to Coxwold (GR 547 785); alternatively there is a layby immediately beside the abbey itself, on a bend in the road where there are two large white gates and a medieval arch. Please do not park in the car park of the Abbey Inn, the landlord of which says he tends to become aggressive with parking ramblers!

Having walked along the road and visited the abbey, founded here in 1177 and noted for, among other things, its medieval floor tiles and beautiful waterleaf capitals, proceed along the road in the direction of Wass as far as the entrance drive to Abbey House on the left (just by the Byland Abbey name-stone). Walk up the drive, turning right through a gate just before the entrance into the grounds of the house and walking along with a wall to your left to another gate into a large meadow. Bear slightly left, but keep on the level ground (there is no clear path), but having passed a small hillock on the left bear left up to a kissing-gate in the top corner of the field. Now bear half-left to a gate in the fence ahead and walk along a clear grassy track to another gate (footpath sign) and a lane.

The hamlet of Wass lies to the right, but our way goes left, up the lane to a gate and on along the stony track. Climb gently to where the track forks, but instead of taking either branch go straight ahead through the kissing-gate signposted Cam Farm and Observatory. Walk forward up the hollowed way with a fence to the left, but in 100 yards, where the path forks, keep right on an ascending path through the bracken. Pass to the right of some gorse bushes and through a line of old hawthorn trees onto a clear track which soon bears slightly right and ascends as a grassy track to a stile into the woods (footpath sign).

In a few yards you reach a track on a bend: keep left here. At the next junction bear right, ie really straight ahead. Ascend to another junction where again you keep right, and follow this track until you emerge from the wood and are faced by a gate with a yellow arrow on it. Ignore this gate and turn left along a grassy track with a wall and fields to your right. Where the track forks keep to the broader, left-hand branch bearing into the wood. The deep ditch to the left of the track is marked Camp Holes on the map. The track leads to the disused observatory where a plaque states that it was erected by John Wormald in the first year of the reign of Queen Victoria, ie 1838.

Stand at the end of the track you have just come by and face the observatory: now walk a yard or two to the left to find on the left a clear but narrow path descending steeply. It leads down through the woods to join a metalled forest road where you turn right. At the next T junction go left and 60 yards further on at the next one left again. Where the track makes a left-hand bend the SHORTER WALK goes left with it and at the next T junction left again into Oldstead (move to * below for the continuation of the route description). The LONGER WALK turns right up the stony track, which is in fact the York branch of the Hambleton Drove Road.

Ignore a track branching right through a gate, but when you reach another large gate on the right with a stile by it and a yellow waymark, pause to admire the view on both sides of the track. Looking over the gate and to the right you will make out the tower of the observatory peeping over the trees; the valley in between is Cocker Dale. Keep forward up the fenced track. Pass through a gate and immediately keep left at the fork. Soon you are on a narrow ascending path. Pass through another gate and reach on the left the memorial chapel built to three men killed in the Second World War. The modern wooden door, carved with a series of Biblical scenes, and the striking stone tympanum above, are admirable. A few yards further on you meet a cross-track. This is Scotch Corner, where the Scots beat the English at the battle of Byland in 1322. Take the left-hand, ascending branch.

When you meet a metalled forest road keep straight ahead along it. The wood continues to your right but there are now fields to the left, and soon the wood ends on the right as well. The track turns left at Shaw's Gate and comes to a motor road. Looking left here you will see to the left of the road a track marked 'Unsuitable for Motors'. This is another branch of the old drove road. Proceed down the track. When you come to a metal gate on the right opposite a stony track on the left, pause again to admire the view: there may be some activity at the gliding club straight ahead, and further left there is a magnificent panorama west and south.

Resume your descent along the track, which from now on is tarmacked. You are joined by a track from the right coming from Silver Fox Farm. At the motor road at the bottom go left to Oldstead.

(*Now the SHORTER and LONGER WALKS rejoin.) Walk along the road towards Oldstead, but just after the first house on the left (Sand

Lane House) fork left along a drive. Cross a cattle grid and walk along an avenue of tall trees, but after a short distance cross a ladder-stile in the fence on the right and follow the direction of the signpost steeply up the bank into a field. You could bear left along the bottom edge of the field and at the next corner bear sharply right uphill, but the right of way cuts this corner by continuing to slant uphill to join the fence higher up. Now follow this fence on your left to cross a double stile in the field corner, and keep on along the fence on your left. The hamlet of Oldstead is a short way off on the right. There is another double stile in the next corner and then a narrow fenced path leads down to a road. The view left still includes the top of the observatory.

Turn right along the road, but only as far as the next farm access road on the left (to Oldstead Grange). The road bears left to pass in front of Wakendale House and the Grange: walk straight through the farmyard to a large gate at the far side (with a yellow waymark). Now fork right on the track descending to the far bottom corner of the field. Pass through another gate and then either turn immediately left up a footpath through trees or follow the track as it bears left round the edge of the field. Both meet up at the top of the hill and bear right with the edge of the field (signpost to Byland Abbey). At the next corner go sharp left, still along the edge of the field, to a stile in the next corner.

Keep forward with the hedge to your left. In the far corner of this field go over the stile on the left and turn right to another stile, then along the bottom edge of two fields with a hedge to the right. Having crossed a stile into the next field, your way lies straight across the middle of it to another stile to the right of a large ash tree. Bear slightly left to pick up the fence/hedge on your left, which you follow along to another stile and the road. The layby where you left the car is a short distance to the right, the abbey a short way to the left.

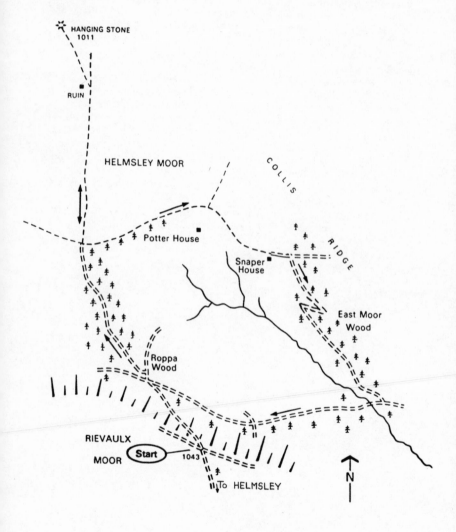

||||||||||||
WALK 18
||||||||||||

HANGING STONE
1011

RUIN

HELMSLEY MOOR

C O L L I S

R I D G E

Potter House

Snaper
House

East Moor
Wood

Roppa
Wood

RIEVAULX

MOOR   Start   1043

To HELMSLEY

N

HELMSLEY BANK

WALK 18

★

4¼ miles (7 km)

To reach the starting point at Helmsley Bank take the road in Helmsley between the church and the Feversham Arms; 200 yards ahead turn left into a No Through Road (leaving the old graveyard on your right) and follow it for 4 miles to its highest point, carefully closing any gates you have to open on the way. Park here on the cropped grass among the heather (GR 590 907).

There is a grand view. Helmsley Bank is on the northern edge of the tabular hills, so characteristic of the whole of the southern boundary of the National Park. The rock beneath our feet is corallian limestone, whereas away to the north the rock is chiefly sandstone, a base on which the heather thrives. Looking north towards the television mast on Bilsdale West Moor, the purple heather on Helmsley Moor below us contrasts with the greens of the forest and the browns of the bracken. Here too are to be seen the remains of a sculpture by Austin Wright, erected in 1977, originally consisting of two large irregular metal 'D's. Its purpose was said to be 'to enhance the view', but it was the subject of controversy and press correspondence.

To the left towards a triangulation pillar and to the right into more forests there are good walks along the edge of the escarpment (see Walk 11), but our route today takes us straight on, sloping to the left down Helmsley Bank from which the whole of the route may be seen: Roppa Wood below, the two farms which will be skirted on the way to East Moor Wood and the trail back through the plantations below and to the right.

At the bottom of the steep slope the tarred road ends at forest cross-tracks, and this is the point to which we shall return via the track on the right. Continue forward over the cross-track for about 30 paces, then bear left onto another track (the track ahead is signposted to Potter House Farm). Your route from Helmsley and now on this forest track has been on the old coach road over the moors to Stokesley, which joins the Bilsdale road just short of Grange. On emerging from the trees the view to the left opens out to reveal Easterside Hill and the moors beyond Bilsdale.

Leave the forest area over a stile by a gate and turn right on a clear track. (You could at this point make an 'out and in' detour straight ahead on a path through the heather marked by a cairn to a group of Bronze

Age tumuli, but the going is rather tough, the path not always clear and the view when you get there is essentially of a sea of heather, so it's really only something for those with a lot of surplus energy!)

The track leads to Potter House Farm, which you will soon see a field's length away to your right. Just past the farm the main track curves away left, but you keep straight on along the fence on your right to the first gate in it. Through this walk forward across the field towards a gate in the wall enclosing the farm infields, but turn left before you reach it on a path which keeps the wall to your right, and when the wall ends bear slightly left away from the fence towards the next farm ahead, Snaper House. Soon you are walking parallel to another wall on your right.

Pass through a gateway at the far end of the field, with the derelict farm to your right, and bear left along the track towards the forest, following the wall on your right, to a gate just where the trees begin. Through it turn right down a track on the edge of the wood. The wood has been devastated by storm damage and there are fallen trees and branches to be negotiated, but there are no problems. There are also very good views of the hills from which we started the walk. When the fence turns right the track goes with it, but in a few yards, opposite a gate on the right (with a Keep Out notice), turn left along a grassy ride. Again fallen trees impede your progress.

Watch out for where the grassy track makes a 180° turn to the right and follow it down to an earth road. Turn left down this, with a valley down to your right. When you reach a metalled (not tarred) road turn right along it over a bridge, and follow it uphill, ignoring side roads. The views open out to the right and eventually the cross-tracks we met on the outward journey will be reached again. Turn left up the hill to return to the car.

HELMSLEY, MONKS' TROD, SHALLOW DALE, AMPLEFORTH AND SPROXTON

WALK 19

★

13 miles (21 km)

The walk starts out along the first 2 km of the Cleveland Way, reveals a glorious variety of scenery, mainly on clear tracks and footpaths, with many distant views, and two charming villages, and returns to Helmsley along the first 4 km of the Ebor Way, the long-distance path which links the Cleveland Way at Helmsley with the Dales Way at Ilkley.

Park in Helmsley, a lovely little Ryedale market town and an ideal holiday centre for the Moors (GR 611 837).

Leave the Market Place by the corner where the National Westminster bank is, and at the T junction, with the parish church to your right, cross the road and turn right. Take the first minor road to the left, signposted 'Footpath to Rievaulx', and leaving the car park to your left walk straight ahead along the stony track (Cleveland Way sign).

When the track ends at a gate cross the stile and turn sharp left down the edge of the field (there is a nice view back to Helmsley Castle at this point). At the foot turn sharp right and continue along the bottom edge of the field. Cross a ladder-stile and keep on along the edge of the next field until you reach a bridle-gate on the left. Go through this and descend gently on the narrow but clear path through the wood. A set of steps leads down a small ravine and up the other side; you then pass through two bridle-gates and reach an open meadow with the 18th century Griff Lodge ahead.

Cross the grass on the clear track to reach a cross-track near the edge of Jinny York Bank, with a fine view of Ryedale, and proceed along the grassy track to the left of Griff Lodge (Cleveland Way signs), over a stile by a gate and along the top edge of Whinny Bank Wood. The track leads to a motor road where you turn left. As you approach Rievaulx Bridge look right for a view of the abbey. Ignore the road to the abbey and cross the bridge, admiring the very beautiful garden of Bridge Cottage on the right. Pass a minor road forking right to Cold Kirby and Old Byland by the whitewashed Ashberry Farm, and just after the next building on the left turn left up a stony track (bridleway sign). You have now left the Cleveland Way.

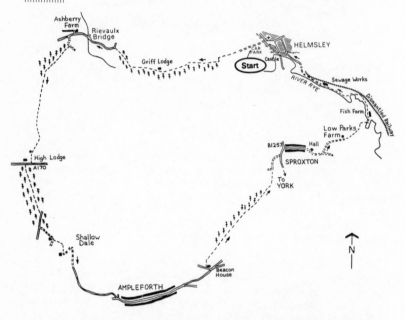

Soon the track bears left. Look left to see above the woodland in the distance the two 18th century temples on Rievaulx Terrace, with the abbey below. Soon you must fork right onto a narrower track up to a bridleway sign and so up into the woods. This bridleway essentially follows the line of the Monks' Trod which linked Rievaulx and Byland Abbeys. Shortly after leaving the wood the track forks: keep right, but when faced by a gate ahead into the wood bear left and then right with the track to pass through a gate. Your route lies straight up the middle of this enormous field (fine views back), passes to the right of two hawthorn trees which are close together and then makes for a stile by a gate which can be seen ahead just to the left of a power line pole.

Now keep forward across another enormous field. This area is Scawton Moor, which before the Second World War was a deer park on the Duncombe Park estate and was then a glorious mass of heather. Pass to the right of a hawthorn copse, cross a stile in the next facing fence and walk straight forward to a bridle-gate ahead. The line of the old Trod, a hollow way, can now clearly be seen. Follow this line (glorious views back) to the next gate, which is a large one, then keep the wire fence on your left to some large barns, where you pass through two more gates onto a stony track which leads to the main road (A170).

60

Cross this busy road with care and turn right along it. Opposite the entrance to High Lodge Farm plunge left into the woods (bridleway sign) along a narrow but reasonably clear path. When you come to a crossing of rides keep straight ahead, now on a clearer track. Ignore the next ride branching left. On reaching a forest road, bear left along it, and at the next junction of tracks bear left to join a motor road. Turn right along it. A sign soon warns of a 1:6 steep hill. A few yards beyond it turn left up a track (footpath sign). Now extensive views open up south.

Pass a shelter belt of trees and the drive on the right to a large house, go through the second of two large gates side by side on the left and walk down the field with the fence to your left. Now comes the only part of the walk where route finding might be tricky and the line of the path not clear: but it doesn't last long. At the bottom of the field, where the fence turns right, the right of way goes straight ahead. At present there is barbed wire here, but a few yards to the left the wire has been cut: cross here and bear right down through the woods and then head-high bracken and brambles, quite steeply in places, to a stile into a large pasture just above a large modernised house. Walk down with the fence on your left to pass to the left of a barn; opposite the entrance to this turn left and walk along near the bottom of the next field to a stile in the fence on your right about 50 yards along. Join the stony access track and turn left. Now your way is straightforward again!

This delightful valley is Shallow Dale. Soon the track becomes tarmacked, and it leads all the way to the main road just outside Ampleforth. There are more fine views on the way (can you see the Pennines?). At the main road turn left to walk straight through the attractive village of Ampleforth, where if your timing is right you will have the opportunity to stop for refreshment. At the far end of the village, 20 yards before the end of the 30 mph limit, join a raised footpath along the left-hand side of the road. Where the road forks keep left (signposted Helmsley 4) and at the top of the hill take the first minor road on the left (signposted Thirsk 12), but immediately after the first house on the right (Beacon House) turn right over the stile (footpath sign) and walk forward with a fence to your right (fine view ahead).

Where the fence bears left at the corner of the field, go over the stile and bear very slightly right across the middle of the next field towards the right-hand corner of the wood ahead. Several of the fields you now pass through may be under crops, but you should always find that the line of the footpath has been restored and is clearly visible. Pass through a gap in the next facing hedge and walk straight over the next field to a stile. Now you follow the right-hand edge of the wood through several more fields. Where the wood ends, bear left with the fence down to the corner of the field (you may have to cross a fence 5 yards before you reach the bottom corner) and turn right along with the fence to your left. At the end of the field which lies on the other side of this fence a tree stump forms a stile: cross this and proceed with a fence to your right to join a tarmacked lane. Bear right along it and at the main road turn left up to Sproxton. This nasty section along a busy road is fortunately short.

At the top of the hill, just before the church, turn right along the No Through Road through the charming, well cared-for backwater of Sproxton, which can even boast a thatched cottage. Continue along the road to pass to the right of Sproxton Hall, now on a stony track, and 200 yards beyond the Hall keep left when the track forks. This is where you join the Ebor Way. When the track bears left to Low Parks Farm keep straight ahead with a fence on your left to a stile by a metal gate. Now keep the fence to your right, soon with a wood on the other side. When you reach a clear track coming from the farm cross straight over and descend a less clear, grassy track to the left-hand corner of the wood ahead where you can see a gate. Cross the stile by the gate and continue along the track with the hedge to your left.

In the bottom corner of the field pass through the gate and bear right down the next field to another gate 30 yards ahead. Now keep forward along the edge of the next field with trees to your right to a metal gate on your right. Through this bear slightly right to cross the river Rye by a footbridge. Turn left along the track by the fish farm. Join a stony track and bear left along it, but where in 40 yards it curves right, keep straight ahead over the stile and on with a deep ditch to your right and soon the river to your left. Pass through a gate and continue with the fence and river to your left, soon however bearing slightly right (waymark) away from the river on a clear path towards the wood ahead. Walk along with the wood on your right for a short distance, but when you reach a gate on the right leading to an old railway tunnel bear half-left to cross a footbridge and go over a stile by a bridle-gate.

Keep straight ahead on a reasonably clear path and bear right along the river bank. Stay with the river until you cross through an old hawthorn hedge, then bear slightly right away from the river towards the fence on the right (the river makes a large loop at this point which we do not need to follow). Follow the fence to a stile in it and proceed along the edge of the field with trees and the river to your left. Follow the river bank, crossing several stiles, until just past the sewage works, where you join a track which leads eventually to the right of a sawmill. Keep left where the track forks; it soon bears left again and you join a tarmacked road into Helmsley. At a T junction turn left, and at the main road by the bridge go right to return to the Market Place.

RICCAL DALE

WALK 20

★

6½ miles (10.5 km)

Riccal Dale is a lovely tree-clad valley, worth a visit at any time of the year but especially beautiful in autumn. In April the banks are bright with primroses, violets, wood anemones and daffodils, to be followed in May by the bluebells. The walk is mainly on forest roads and tracks, with occasional stretches which can be muddy. A feature of the rivers and streams coming down from the moors and cutting through the tabular hills is that in dry weather they sink below the stream bed and come up again at kelds a mile or more lower down. The river Riccal is no exception: it is quite probable a walker will find the river bed dry at the beginning of the walk but full of rippling water higher up the valley.

Take the A170 Kirkbymoorside road out of Helmsley and after a little more than a mile park the car on the grass verge on the left just before the first bridge (Riccal Bridge GR 633 842), taking care not to block the gateway.

Go over the stile by the gate (public footpath sign) and follow the track, crossing another stile by another gate on the way.

In dry weather the following short variant can be made (but it is perfectly pleasant to stay on the forest road): shortly after you pass a minor track forking left and another one descending right, the forest road bears gently left, and on this bend find a narrow path on the right descending to a footbridge. Cross this and bear slightly left, walking forward on a narrow path with the river to your left. When you reach a grassy track, turn left along it. Quite soon the track leads you back over the river at a ford, easy to cross except after rain.

Continue on the track through the trees with the river to your right. The track leads out into a field and bears left, soon to re-enter the trees. The forest road is only a few yards off to the left. The track passes along the left-hand edge of another grassy glade, then bears left to rejoin the forest road.

Continue along the forest road, soon to be joined by another one descending from the left. At times you are walking at river level, at others high above it. Having been up high for a stretch and descended to river level again, a metalled road on the right leads past a wooden hut to a concrete bridge, a pleasant spot for a picnic, but return to the road which you have been following and continue up-valley, either keeping on the road or, another short diversion which although attractive can be very wet, in a few

63

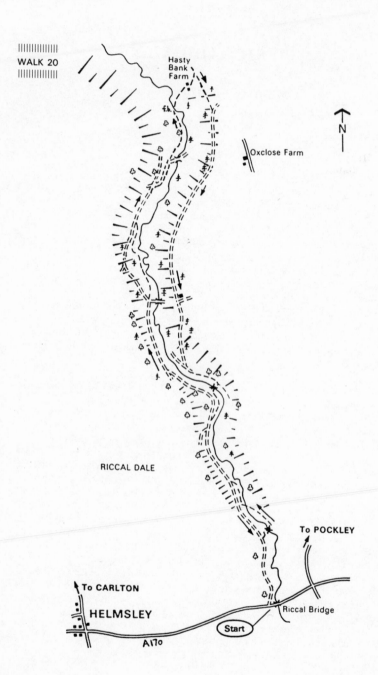

WALK 20

Hasty Bank Farm

Oxclose Farm

N

RICCAL DALE

To POCKLEY

To CARLTON

HELMSLEY

Riccal Bridge

Start

A170

64

yards forking right off the road along a grassy track through the trees.

[If you elect to stay on the road, skip this paragraph:] A fallen tree blocks the way at present (1991), but make your way round it and continue on the track with the river to your right. After crossing a small side-stream the track bears left through the trees, and soon the river is back on your right and the track is reduced to a narrow footpath. Again there are fallen branches to negotiate and the path can be muddy. Just before you reach the vestiges of a red-brick building in the trees (on the far side of a side-stream), bear left and clamber up the bank to rejoin the forest road.

[If you stay on the forest road instead of making that diversion, you will climb, be joined at the top by another road from the left and descend again.] Continue along the forest road until it forks (at a point where there is also a minor track coming in from the left) and go right. At the next fork a little later take the left-hand branch (the right-hand one crosses the river by a bridge). Soon there is grass in the middle of the track. Pass round a gate across the track.

When you reach a large open grassy area where there has been some new tree planting and where there are three wooden buildings, bear slightly left off the main track and walk along the length of the glade, soon to re-enter the trees, now on a grassy path. Pass through a bridle-gate, and across the valley to your right you will see the red roofs of Hasty Bank Farm, your next objective. A track leads to a footbridge, after which it bears left, to pass to the right of the farm outbuildings, through a gate, and immediately to the left of the farmhouse. Two hundred yards past the farm turn right at a fork and continue climbing. Look back as you climb for a good view across the countryside.

Just after passing a small abandoned quarry on the left, the track bears left and levels out. Leave it, to go through the gate on the right and along a grassy track along the top edge of the wood. Oxclose Farm is a field away on the left. If you are walking in April, you will soon pass a glorious spread of daffodils, growing even across your track. Just after you begin to get a view ahead to the Wolds across the Vale of Pickering, the track bears right and begins to descend, but only for 50 yards, before you bear left again and continue on the contouring track through the woods.

Immediately past a wooden pheasant-rearing house on wheels ignore the track going left and take the clear one straight ahead downhill. Soon another track comes in from the left and at the same point a path forks off left: ignore these and keep on the main, descending track. Nearly at the valley bottom, turn left on a cross-track and go through a gate, a clearing and another gate. (The forest road you used earlier is just across the river.) Keep on the good green track until you reach a metal footbridge over the river. Cross this and turn left along the track. In a few yards don't re-cross the river at the ford, but bear right with the track.

The track leads back to the forest road used on your outward route. Turn left along it, keeping left of course at the fork which faces you, to return to the car.

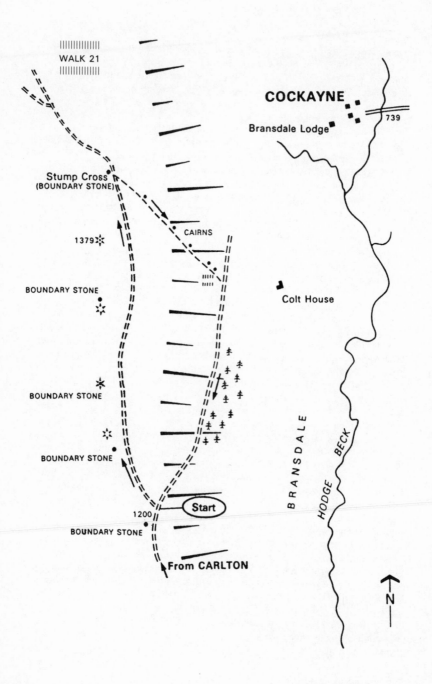

WALK 21

COCKAYNE

Bransdale Lodge

739

Stump Cross
(BOUNDARY STONE)

CAIRNS

Colt House

1379

BOUNDARY STONE

BOUNDARY STONE

BOUNDARY STONE

Start

1200

BOUNDARY STONE

From CARLTON

B R A N S D A L E

H O D G E   B E C K

N

STUMP CROSS AND BRANSDALE

WALK 21

★

2½ miles (4 km)
With an optional extra at Cowhouse Bank
of any distance up to 8 miles (13 km)

The chief aim today is to take a moorland walk along good tracks to a position giving extensive views of the high moors and closer views of Bransdale.

Motoring out of Helmsley on the A170 Scarborough (Kirkbymoorside) road, before reaching the end of the houses turn left for the pretty village of Carlton. At 1.3 miles to the north of Carlton the road reaches a very fine viewpoint at Cowhouse Bank, so before continuing towards Bransdale by car, turn in to the left where there is a signpost which reads 'Footpath to Newgate Bank'. There is plenty of room to park the car. (GR 614 886). This is another of those places on the edge of the tabular hills always worth pausing at for the extensive views they give to the north. To the left front is Helmsley Moor with Roppa Plantation below it and East Moor Wood to the right of that. Above the trees straight ahead are the moors of Bransdale: East Moors, Pockley Moor, both of which we shall cross by car, and Bilsdale East Moor, on which we shall be walking shortly. Over to the right is Birk Nab and the valley still further to the right is Riccal Dale.

The walk of the day being only a short one, the reader may be tempted to investigate the footpath indicated by the signpost, all of it being on good forest roads and tracks, giving many good views over the escarpment. The rule is: keep to the path along the edge and do not go downhill. For the full distance, walk to the sculpture on the top of Helmsley Bank (Walk 18) and from there follow the route of Walk 11, starting in the second last paragraph, to Newgate Bank and back, returning by the same route from Helmsley Bank to Cowhouse Bank.

Resuming the car journey, go down Cowhouse Bank and enjoy the moorland drive until the top end of Bransdale comes in sight; 5.4 miles from Cowhouse Bank, just before the road turns downhill, there is a signpost on the left saying 'Bridleway to Bilsdale'. Leave the car here (GR 609 963).

Set out along the good moorland track. In a yard or two you pass a stone telling you that you are walking on the Nawton Tower Estate, and a little further a sign indicating no access for motor vehicles. On the left as you walk you will pass bumps and stones of various shapes and sizes: some are tumuli, others boundary stones and others combinations of both. Those interested will find that all the cairns have been opened up. It was probably done during the 19th century when there was a spate of digging of these ancient burial mounds which, although originally erected in the Bronze Age, were often found to contain the remains of people who lived in later centuries as well as the original bones.

Almost at the end of a long, gentle left-hand curve you will come across the Stump Cross, the base of an old cross which marked a corner of the parish boundary; well, not so much a corner as a slight change of direction. Just north of the cross the view really opens out. Walk on for about 300 yards from the cross to where the footpath to Tripsdale bears to the left and pause to have a look around. The depression down to the left is Tarn Hole; the track swinging round to the west to Tripsdale goes on to Bilsdale, but Tripsdale is out of sight below the line of the moor. Parts of Bilsdale can be seen with Cringle Moor and Carlton Moor beyond. The bulldozed route to the north points to the white trig point on Round Hill at Botton Head, at 1,489 ft above sea level the highest point on the North York Moors. Over to the east are the moors above Bransdale, Farndale and Rosedale.

Return to Stump Cross. Some 20 yards beyond it, on the left-hand side of the track, there is a small cairn, and a few yards into the heather another one; a third cairn can be seen some way ahead. This is the line of your descent. Follow the clear, cairned path as far as the last, somewhat larger cairn, where the path forks. Keep left here, heading straight down the hillside. In a few yards the path picks up the line of a hollow way, which you follow down to the road, reaching it by some old workings and a signpost pointing back to Bilsdale.

Turn right up the road and walk for nearly a mile back to the car. The short grass by the side of the road is good for walking on and an opportunity may be taken to take a closer look at Bransdale. The view later becomes restricted because of a plantation of larch trees but it opens out again just as the walker is beginning to puff a little before reaching the car at the top of the hill.

COCKAYNE, BLOWORTH CROSSING AND THE RUDLAND RIGG ROAD

WALK 22

★

6½ miles (10.5 km)

For a dry-foot walk, leading at an easy gradient to the high moors at a famous junction of two equally famous routes, one an ancient road the other a disused high level railway track, this would be difficult to beat. Bloworth Crossing is now known to thousands of long-distance walkers every year. The old ironstone railway track at this point is utilised by Lyke Wake walkers; people on the Cleveland Way reach this crossing from the west and then turn north; and walkers on the White Rose Walk may follow the route of the Cleveland Way, or they may cut across the line of the boundary stones which can be seen from here to the north-west.

Cockayne is a small community at the head of Bransdale, hardly big enough to be called a hamlet, beautifully situated among trees and as remote from the bustle of the towns as anywhere in England. It can be reached from Helmsley via Carlton and Cowhouse Bank or from Kirkbymoorside via Fadmoor. *Coming from Helmsley,* drive all the way to the head of the dale. Turn right at the T junction (left leads only to the church of St Nicholas and Bransdale Lodge), descend to cross the bridge and climb steeply up the other side. The road bends sharp right and then sharp left again. Here there is room to park a couple of cars, but please don't obstruct the gates. Alternatively drive on round the next right-hand bend, to where room will be found to park on the verge. *Coming from Kirkbymoorside,* having crossed the moors you find yourself looking down a steep hill into Bransdale; ahead of you, on this side of the valley, you will see a row of farms. You are going to park just beyond the last farm, but well before the forest behind them. Descend across the cattle-grid with the National Trust sign for Bransdale and follow the road up the valley until shortly after the last farm there is a public bridleway sign on the right. There is room to park on the left-hand verge here, or drive a little further to find another suitable spot on the left (GR 623 984).

Having parked, walk back (or forward) towards the head of the valley, and where the road turns sharp left to descend steeply (20%) and cross the stream, go through the gate ahead and follow the track across a field and into the woods. Now follow the good forest road ahead for more than

69

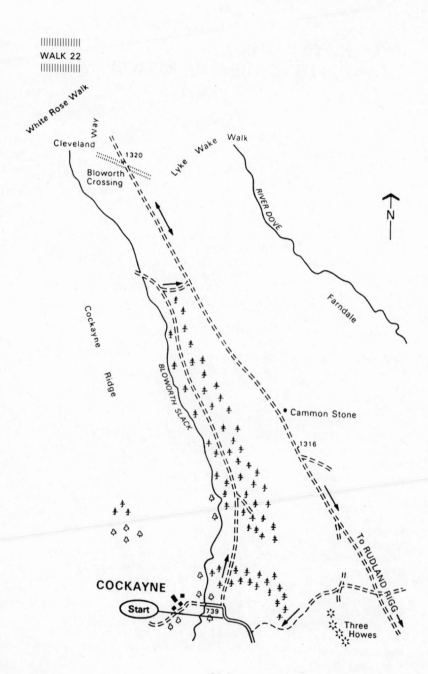

||||||||||||||
WALK 22
||||||||||||||

White Rose Walk

Cleveland

Way

1320

Bloworth
Crossing

Lyke Wake Walk

RIVER DOVE

N

Farndale

Cockayne

Ridge

BLOWORTH SLACK

Cammon Stone

1316

To RUDLAND RIGG

COCKAYNE

Start

739

Three
Howes

a mile until the trees on the right end and the road makes a sharp right-hand curve. Follow it round and up, and looking back up the valley if the weather is clear you should see the line of the old railway just below the brow of the moor; it is also apparent that the top part of the forest you have just walked through has been devastated by storm damage.

The clear cross-track at the top of the hill is the Rudland Rigg road. Rudland Rigg itself lies to the right, dividing Bransdale from Farndale. Five miles to the south, where the road we are on leaves the Fadmoor-Bransdale road, a signpost shows that Stokesley is 16 miles away and another one reads 'Unfit for Motor Vehicles'. May it remain so for ever.

Turn left for the diversion to Bloworth Crossing which can be seen ½ mile away. At Bloworth Crossing the owners of the site of the old railway line have managed to keep motor vehicles off it by putting a locked gate across. The line, which linked Rosedale with Battersby and Middlesborough, carried iron ore across the moors to a height of 1,400 ft above sea level and was the second highest railway in the country.

Now return the way you have come along the Rudland Rigg road. Upper Farndale comes into view on the left and above it the twisting railway track contouring round the head of the valley on Farndale Moor. On Westerdale Moor beyond, a depression leading away to the north shows the position of Esklets in the valley where are the gathering grounds of the streams forming the source of the river Esk, which finds its way to the sea at Whitby. To our right there is a glorious view down Bransdale. Ahead on the left of the road will be seen the Cammon Stone, a big upright stone on the parish boundary. (The Hebrew inscription, likely to be the work of a local vicar in the 19th century, means 'Hallelujah'.) Two hundred yards beyond it there is a green track to the left which is useful if you want to have a closer look at the top end of Farndale.

Continuing south one can see ahead, to the right of the road, the Three Howes, a group of Bronze Age burial cairns; in fact there is another tumulus nearby making four bumps in all. Ignore a grassy track forking off right in the direction of the Howes, and keep on your road until you reach a clear cross-track marked by cairns shortly before the Howes. Turn sharp right on a clear track slanting back through the heather. After some time the track bears left and drops to the left-hand end of a plantation, becoming a hollow way. From the wood the path continues forward towards the wall ahead but bears right down the nearside of it, keeping in the hollow way, which leads to a gate. Pass through and continue in the groove, which bears left and leads to a stile by a gate out onto the road, by a public bridleway sign. The car is either here or along the road to the right.

||||||||||||||
WALK 23
||||||||||||||

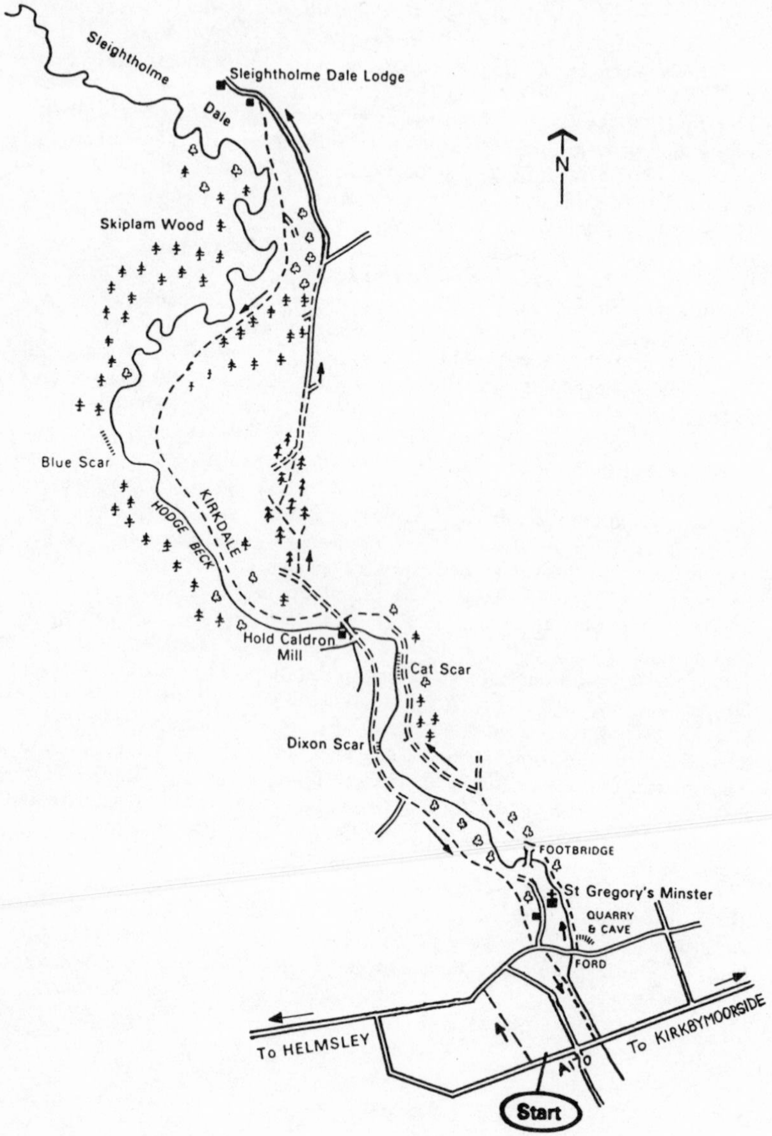

Sleightholme

Dale

Sleightholme Dale Lodge

Skiplam Wood

N

Blue Scar

KIRKDALE

HODGE BECK

Hold Caldron
Mill

Cat Scar

Dixon Scar

FOOTBRIDGE

St Gregory's Minster

QUARRY
& CAVE

FORD

To HELMSLEY

A170

To KIRKBYMOORSIDE

Start

KIRKDALE AND
SLEIGHTHOLME DALE

WALK 23

★

7½ miles (12 km)

Hodge Beck passes through three dales before it leaves the moorland area, first through Bransdale, then as it forces its way through the tabular hills it enters Sleightholme Dale and Kirkdale in quick succession. In fact the two are really one valley, separated merely by a bend in the river round the nab embracing Skiplam Wood. Both are well wooded; Sleightholme Dale is broader and more associated with the moorland.

Part of Kirkdale is just outside the National Park but it is famous for three things: St Gregory's Minster, a cave, and wild lily of the valley.

The little church dates from pre-Conquest times; the sundial is of particularly great interest. But whether or not you are interested in architecture you will certainly be charmed by the setting of this lovely church in the valley.

If you approach Kirkdale *from Helmsley,* drive for 4.6 miles along the A170, ignoring a minor road forking left to St Gregory's Minster and Kirkdale and parking in an old loop of the road which forms a long layby on the left just after the road makes a left-hand bend. If coming *from Kirkbymoorside,* from the roundabout drive for 1.6 miles on the A170 until shortly after a crossroads (Welburn to the left, Kirkdale to the right), then turn into the long layby which of course is now on the right (GR 677 848).

Walk to the Helmsley end of the layby and 20 yards further on go through the gate on the right (bridleway sign). Walk along the right-hand edge of the fields (no path) until another gate gives access to a minor road, along which you turn right. Ignore a road forking right to Welburn, and at the foot of the steep hill fork left for a visit to St Gregory's Minster, then return to this point and continue downhill to cross Hodge Beck by the footbridge beside the ford. Immediately after the bridge turn left along the footpath, but after a few yards fork right onto another path which leads to the quarry where a cave was discovered in 1821 in which were the remains of lion, hyena, mammoth, rhinoceros and other mammals of former periods in our history. The cave is high on the cliff face; if you are a climber and a caver you will be able to scramble up and see two passages through the 2 ft high entrance. Proper equipment would be needed for a full exploration.

Now return to the footpath beside the bridge and walk along it with the beck to your left. When the path forks, keep right, steeply ascending; there are several fallen trees to be negotiated but the path is always clear. For a short distance you contour at some height above the beck, before descending steeply straight down the slope to a level shelf about halfway down where the path bears right and contours again, still some way above the beck. At the first opportunity drop steeply left down to a meadow. There is a footbridge to the left, but turn right along the edge of the field with the wood to your right. Pass through a gate into the wood; in 50 yards ignore a track forking sharply back right. Soon you reach an open space with a gate on the left and a fork in the path ahead: take the left fork straight ahead up into the wood. A few yards further on again take the left fork. The clear path keeps quite close to the left-hand edge of the wood, but soon leaves it and continues with the wood to your right and a fence to your left.

Soon the path, now a clear track, re-enters the wood. When it ascends there are nice views of the dale. At this part of the river there are sink holes in the limestone bed (as in Riccal Dale). For many months of the year the stream bed is dry below here to well below the starting point of the walk. Cross a stile by a gate with Hold Caldron Mill to the left, but turn right along the track. In 100 yards notice a gate on the left, through which you will return later, but for the time being continue along the track. Pass through a gate across it and in 30 yards fork right off the track on a clear path, ascending gently. At the next fork keep left on a good ascending track, and at the next fork keep right, still climbing. The track narrows to a path, but near the top edge of the wood you meet a cross-track along which you turn right. Ignore a path forking right and walk along a few yards from the left-hand edge of the wood.

Leave the wood and keep forward on the grassy track with a hedge to your right. Where the track forks keep left, now with a hedge on both sides. When you reach a motor-road turn left to slope downhill through deciduous woods. Immediately before the first building you reach on the left, a stone garage, turn sharp left along a track, passing a sign 'Footpath to Hold Caldron'. There are fine views back right past Sleightholme Dale Lodge up the valley. Ignore a track forking right to a gate, but a few yards further on keep right at a fork on the lower track. Ignore another track forking right to a gate and keep left, now on a narrower path, still just inside the wood. Soon you cross through the middle of a piece of woodland before returning to the edge of the wood. Now ignore all temptations to leave it and keep on the path just inside the wood until you can follow it no further and must cross a stile. Bear left along the grassy track. At the end of the field continue on the broad track with the beck just to your right. Pass through a gate and keep forward on the grassy track. The next gate is the one you passed earlier: cross the stile beside it and bear right along the track, but this time keep bearing right to cross the bridge and pass Hold Caldron Mill.

Follow the tarmacked road. Pass an old limekiln on the way up, and at the top of the hill go through the gate on the left (bridleway sign). The path is narrow and overgrown and rather uncomfortable if you are wearing shorts! But keep a sharp lookout for where a path forks right to a bridle-gate into a field. Don't miss it! Bear left along the left-hand edge of the field with the wood to your left. Pass through another bridle-gate and follow the edge of the field, at one point there is a fine view of the Minster, until you reach a white gate in the fence on the left. Go through and drop steeply to the road.

Again walk down the road towards the ford, but this time only for a few yards to another white gate on the right (footpath sign). Once in the field bear left, soon cutting a corner to continue forward with the fence to your left. Soon there is a wood to your left and a steep bank. At the end of the field cross an old railway track and keep on with the fence/hedge to your left until you reach another white gate which gives access to the main road. Turn right along the wide verge to return to the car.

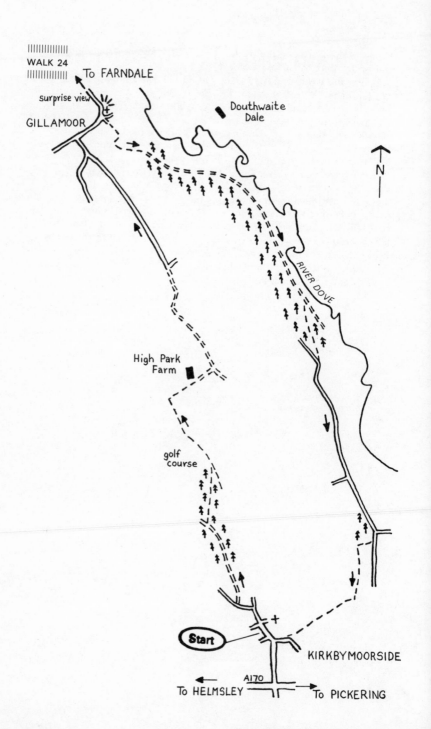

||||||||||||
WALK 24
||||||||||||

To FARNDALE

surprise view

GILLAMOOR

Douthwaite Dale

N

River Dove

High Park Farm

golf course

Start

KIRKBYMOORSIDE

A170

To HELMSLEY

To PICKERING

KIRKBYMOORSIDE, GILLAMOOR
AND DOUTHWAITE DALE

WALK 24

★

5 miles (8 km)

A gentle stroll on easy paths and tracks to a superb viewpoint, returning along a quiet valley, with one or two overgrown sections which give a mild sense of adventure.

There is no shortage of parking space in Kirkbymoorside.

Walk up to the top of the Market Place and then its continuation, High Market Place, to the mini-roundabout at the top. Here turn left, but take the first minor road on the right, signposted to the NYCC depot and the golf course. Walk through the County Council's Highways Depot and continue up the stony road. Three yards after the better tarmac surface starts, fork right off the road (footpath sign) up a clear footpath. Towards the top of the wood ignore several paths forking right, and when faced by a fence and fields ahead turn left along the clear cross-path just to the left of a large ash tree.

The path follows the left-hand edge of a large field, with the golf course audible but largely invisible over the hedge. The path bears right, still following the hedge, to reach High Park Farm, where it goes through a gate on the left and then bears right along the concrete access road. At the T junction, when the concreting ends, turn left along the stony track, and follow this track/road all the way to Gillamoor, the moors ahead coming closer with every step. On reaching the main road, keep forward into the village and at the T junction turn right along the village street, bearing left with the main road at the war memorial to reach the Surprise View. The sight of dale and rolling moorland can be breathtaking. Time and time again the author has visited this spot, never failing to read the inscription on the churchyard wall near the conveniently placed seat:

> Thou, who hast given me eyes to see
> And love this sight so fair,
> Give me a heart to find out Thee
> And read Thee everywhere.
>
> J. Keble

Return towards the village, but turn left immediately beyond the churchyard wall to cross the green and two tarmacked paths, one leading to the church, the other to a garage on the left. Keep forward to pass through a gate (footpath sign) onto a narrow overgrown path. On passing under some power lines look left for a fine view over Douthwaite Dale. The path crosses the head of a shallow valley dropping left and there are a few more overgrown yards before you reach a gate into a field. Cross the field diagonally left to the far corner where a gate leads to a path down through the woods, a deeply hollowed way, clearly a route of some antiquity. Pass through a gate out of the wood and keep forward to the right of an ancient hedge. Douthwaite Dale is to the left. Ignore a gate on the right leading back into the woods and make for the one straight ahead. The clear track continues forward, soon with a fence to the left and the wood to the right.

Just before the next gate ignore the fork to the right, pass through the gate and continue forward with the wood to the right. The broad level track contours along the side of the valley, it is called 'Shepherd's Road' on the map, until another gate readmits you to the wood. At the next fork keep left. Soon you are joined by another track coming in from the left and now you must watch out! Pass a gate on the left into a field; 40 yards past it look out for an indistinct path forking right off the track. The gap through the trees which the path follows up is clear, but the path itself is heavily overgrown. Soon however you are in a narrow hollow way, clearly used by horses as it can be muddy.

When you reach a clear cross-track go left, but in a few yards fork right and continue uphill. When the path levels out again fork right, leave the wood (bridleway sign) and turn left along the track. When you reach a tarmacked road bear left, and 50 yards after you are joined by another tarmacked road coming from the left go through a kissing-gate on the right (footpath sign) at the far end of a wood and walk up the field with the wood to your right. At the top go through another kissing-gate and turn left along the field edge. When you are faced by a wood ahead, turn right for 30 yards with the wood to your left, then sharp left again. At the end of the field cross the stile and continue downhill still with the wood to your left. Kirkbymoorside is ahead. Cross a stile into a children's playground and follow the hedge on the right down to the road. Keep straight ahead to return to the Market Place.

LOWNA AND LOWER FARNDALE

WALK 25

★

5 miles (8 km)

This is a delightful and easy ramble mainly on old tracks, often through woods rich in wildlife, with lovely views. Occasionally attention must be paid to route finding, and in late summer some short sections may be overgrown.

Farndale may be approached from the north via Castleton, from the south-east via Hutton-le-Hole and from the south-west through Gillamoor. All the roads are good for the motorist but the best is the last one — simply for the benefit of the Surprise View at Gillamoor (see Walk 24).

From the Surprise View continue down the road into Farndale. Just after passing the road to Low Mill on the left a public car park is signposted, also on the left. Park here (GR 685 910). If the car park is full continue down the road and cross Lowna bridge: there is roadside parking on the right, or where a stony road on the left joins the motor road.

From the far end of the official car park walk along the grassy lane which leads down to a footbridge over a stream. Cross this and bear right on the clear path. Presently you come to a fork by a Farndale Nature Reserve sign: follow the left-hand branch signposted to Low Mill via Park Farm. Soon on the left you pass a walled enclosure and a plaque informs you that this was the Quaker Burial Ground of Lowna, in use from 1675 to 1837. Continue through the bracken. The clear path, never far from the wall on the right, eventually leads through a gate into a conifer plantation. Keep straight ahead on the track through the wood, which has suffered much through storm damage, leaving it again at the far end through a gateway and continuing forward on a clear track, with fine views of the valley to the right.

When the track forks keep right, and in a few yards join a much clearer track coming down the hillside from the left. Turn right along it (lovely view of Farndale ahead), pass through a gate saying 'Beware Bull', then another gate, then straight through the farmyard of Park Farm to a wooden gate at the far end. Keep forward with the wall to your left, and where it ends head straight across the next rough pasture. When you reach the hedge at the far side, bear left up it, keeping the hedge to your right, and now you are back on a track. Pass through a gate at the top and bear right with the track. Keep the wall/fence/wall to your right and the track becomes clear through the bracken. You are still contouring,

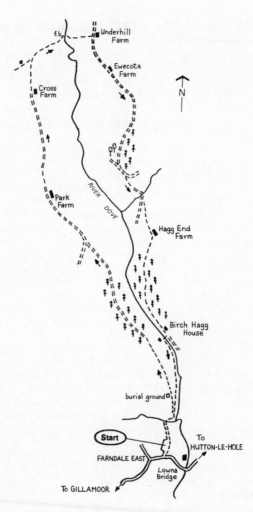

with good views right over Farndale. The track leads round the top side of Cross Farm.

Now take care over route finding! Bear right at the far end of the buildings, crossing a footpath coming from the farm and dropping to a track also coming from the buildings. Turn left along it to a large gate ahead with a yellow waymark. Through this bear half-right diagonally across the next large field, but when you are level with the nearside of the garden enclosure of the house up to the left you will see a faint grassy track coming straight down the hillside past the garden wall. Turn right

80

on it down the slope, pass through the remains of the hedge of the field you are in, and in a few yards fork left off the track (which leads down to a gate ahead) on a faint path to a plank bridge and stile in the facing hedge (30 yards to the left of that gate).

Now route finding is straightforward again! Walk down the next field on a faint path, keeping the hedge to your right, to a stile in the bottom corner (there is a yellow arrow on the tree next to the stile). In the next field still keep the hedge to your right, and soon you will see a stile in the fence at the bottom of the field a few yards to the left of the corner. Cross it and follow the faint path straight downhill, bearing left when you reach the river Dove, which you cross in a few yards by a footbridge. Walk straight forward across the rushy field and up the bank to the fence, turning right along it; it soon bears left and leads you uphill to Underhill Farm (lovely view back as you climb). Go through the gate at the top and turn right along the hedged track in front of the farm.

The next section can be very overgrown. Pass through another facing gate and continue up the lane (it is in fact an old unclassified country road) to Ewecote Farm. Walk straight forward through the farmyard and on along the hedged lane at the far side. Pass through another gate and continue along the grassy lane. After another gate you are again walking through bracken with a wood to the left. After another gate you have the wood on both sides. When you reach a farm access track turn left along it for a few yards then fork right off it on a clear path. Soon a stretch of duckboarding helps you over a very wet section. Continue along the old broad walled lane, soon passing through another gate and bearing right to cross a stream by a clapper bridge.

Twenty yards further on go through a gate in the wall on the left and walk straight across the field to another gate at the far side. Follow the wall on your left to another gate, then keep forward to Hagg End Farm, where you pass to the right of all the buildings to reach a gate. Walk along the next field with a wall to your left to a gateway ahead. Now walk straight across the next field to a gate into the wood ahead. Follow the clear path through the wood, from which you emerge by another gate. Pass to the right of the garden and house of Birch Hagg, then bear right over the broad wooden bridge. Turn left in front of the stone barn, pass through a gate and walk through the next field with the river to your left. A clear path soon develops. Pass through a gate and continue with the river to your left. If you are here in April you will enjoy the daffodils.

Cross a stile by a gate and keep forward along the path, soon bearing right with a stream to your left, to reach the footpath signpost you passed on the outward journey. Keep forward with the stream to your left, cross it by the footbridge, and return up the lane to the car.

THE FARNDALE DAFFODIL ROUTE

WALK 26

★

3 miles (5 km) or 7 miles (11 km)

Farndale is lovely at any time of the year, but the best time to visit it is when the famous wild daffodils are in full bloom, spreading a yellow carpet on the valley bottom and alongside the streams. Depending on the seasons, usually the most rewarding time to see the daffodils is from the middle to the end of April, and although the blooms are spread all along the river Dove the classic route for walkers is between the hamlets of Low Mill and Church Houses, the first 1½ miles of today's journey. For those who only want to stroll, stand and stare, to return by the outward route will present no hardship, but there will be some, looking for more exercise, who will welcome a visit to the moors and the subsequent drop down to West Gill, a peaceful place. NOTE: in the daffodil season Farndale gets very crowded and weekends are best avoided.

Low Mill is a little more than 3 miles up the dale from Gillamoor and a little less than 4 from Hutton-le-Hole, and the free car park is in the centre of the village (GR 673 953). Here there are toilets and in the season a National Park information caravan. When the daffodils are in bloom the car park soon fills up, but the owner of the adjoining field opens it to motors at a small charge.

From the car park take the path signposted to High Mill, through the gate, down the paved path to a footbridge over the stream. Turn left and you are immediately among the flowers which, as you will have read on the Nature Reserve signs, must not be picked. The river is quite wide at this point and on the whole of the daffodil route the path is on the east side of it, well marked by constant use and supplied with good stiles and footbridges all the way. The footbridges are needed only to cross the side streams. When you have walked, strolled and loitered for 1½ miles you will reach the buildings of High Mill. You can either turn back here or go through the gate, follow the track between the buildings and enter the lane to Church Houses.

The hill ahead of you is Potter's Nab, with High Blakey Moor behind it. When you reach Church Houses turn immediately left on the motor road, before the Feversham Arms. It is busy in the season but there is only ½ mile of it before the junction is reached at the top of the hill. Turn right (signposted to Dale End west only) and pass through a gateway immediately above the derelict Monket House. Straight away

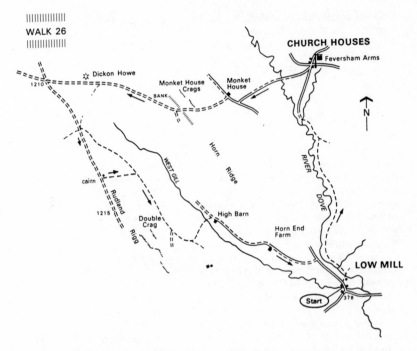

turn left through a gate onto a stony track which rapidly rises through
spoil heaps and crags. Ignoring side roads or tracks to left or right and
enjoying the views down into upper Farndale, continue on this good
walking road until the major crossroad of Rudland Rigg is reached.
Ahead to the right will be seen one of the Three Howes which are passed
on the other side on Walk 22 and straight ahead, beyond Bransdale and
Bilsdale, is the ever present TV mast.

Turn sharp left here, taking the Rudland Rigg road, first bending to
the left, then to the right, on this road which on most of its length is as
straight as an arrow. To the left there are views across Farndale to Blakey
Ridge where on a clear day the inn can be seen and the road leading up
to it from Church Houses. Nearer, there is Horn Ridge, and dipping
down on this side of it, West Gill, our next objective.

Now comes the only place on this walk where you must pay great
attention to route finding. After about 600 yards on the Rudland Rigg
road you will reach a metal post on the left (there is also a wooden market
post on the right) which marks the start of the bridleway down into West
Gill. But as the first section of the bridleway is not clear on the ground
and crosses tough heather moorland, we shall continue on the road and
use an unofficial footpath link to the bridleway further on. So keep on the

road for about another 500 yards, watching out for a small but well made cairn on the left which marks the start of a narrow but well-used path through the heather. It is essential to find this, but having found it your route-finding problems are over.

The path soon begins to descend, giving good views over West Gill, and joins the bridleway at a marker post. Keep slanting down the hillside: the path is clear, but the heather can be high. Shortly after passing another reassuring marker post the path forks. Take the left-hand branch which descends with a gulley to the left. Looking down into the valley below, one can see a barn on the other side of the stream, beyond some trees; the next objective is to cross the stream 200 yards upstream from the barn (High Barn). The path is now fairly level, with a row of crags to the right and the valley to the left. Eventually it descends and takes you through a gate in a wall. Continue forward down the hollow way which soon bears left (marker post) and goes straight down the hill. When the hollow way ends the path bears slightly left and takes you back through the wall over a stile by a gate. Keep downhill, parallel to the wall on your right, to cross the stream.

Turn right onto a cart road which passes the barn and leads to Horn End Farm. Here keep straight ahead, leaving the farm to your right, through a gate and down the farm road. At the junction with the narrow motor road below, a signpost reads 'Bridleway to Rudland Rigg'. Turn right on the road; looking down through the trees, the river Dove will be seen and the daffodils first noticed on the outward route. There were no daffodils in West Gill but it is nevertheless a delightful place of pastoral peace — often in marked contrast to the wind and ruggedness of the surrounding moors. About 400 yards of road walking brings one back to Low Mill.

FARNDALE – A DALE END WALK

WALK 27

★

2½ miles (4 km)

Sometimes it may happen that on arrival in Farndale the daffodils are beginning to fade, either because of an early season or because one is just too late in getting there! It is therefore comforting to know that higher up the valley the flowers bloom later. The walk now being suggested takes one to both sides of the dale at the top end, and when crossing the river both ways one comes across some lovely little corners among trees bearing a mass of daffodils. As in the rest of Farndale, there is really no out-of-season for this country, lovely at any time, beneath the moors. The only uphill work to speak of will be seen from the car before setting off.

Go by car to Church Houses and continue on the road signposted 'Dale End Only'; it leads to the top end of the valley on the east side. Soon, looking down to the left, you will see the beautiful part of the dale in which a few years ago it was proposed to build a reservoir. The narrow road takes us about 2 miles further up the dale before reaching Esk House, a farm where there is a public footpath sign on the left. Note this as you pass it, as this is where you will emerge onto the road on the return journey, and continue by car up the steep hill. Soon after the road begins to descend again, just before a left-hand bend, there is a suitable layby for parking on the right. Leave the car here (GR 644 003).

Continue down the road and cross the bridge over Gill Beck at the bottom; this is quite a beauty spot. A signpost which reads 'Bridle Road to Bloworth' points up the valley. Before the sign is a green lane on the left leading down to the river. After the double walled part of the lane ends, continue downhill, first with a stream to your left, then to your right. The wall on your left leads you through a gate and you cross the river Dove by a good stone footbridge. You may wish to linger in this pleasant place among the trees before continuing up the lane on the other side.

At a clear cross-track turn left: you are now on the road on the west side of the dale. Here it is a rough track and just right for walking on. Pass the access roads to Spout House and Ewe Hill Farms (both sadly derelict) on the left, and follow the track gently uphill. On the brow there is a public footpath sign on each side. Go through the gate on the left and follow the wall down to Wether Hill Farm. Pass to the left of this to find a gate on the right giving access to the farmyard. Through this bear half-

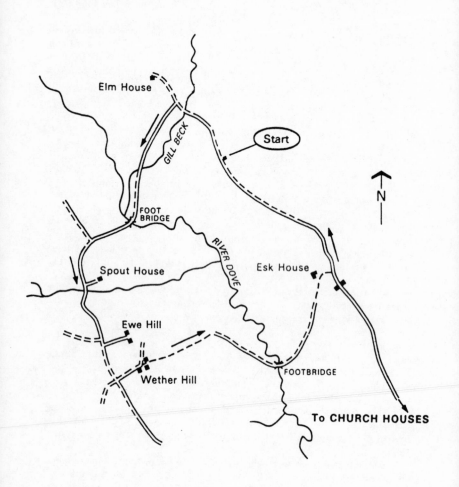

left diagonally down through the yard to a gate in the bottom right-hand corner. Walk straight down the field, parallel to the fence on the left, to a gateway in the wall ahead, then keep forward to the next facing gate. Through this, bear right along with the wall to your right, and where this ends and the fence goes right, keep ahead on the same line across the field to the far corner. There is a carpet of daffodils in the valley bottom in season.

Cross the stile in the corner of the field and walk forward to cross the river by a footbridge. Follow the fence/stream on your right up to a stile by a gate, then continue up the track to Esk House Farm. Walk through the farmyard and bear right to join the motor road at the public footpath sign seen before leaving the car. Turn left along it to return to the starting point.

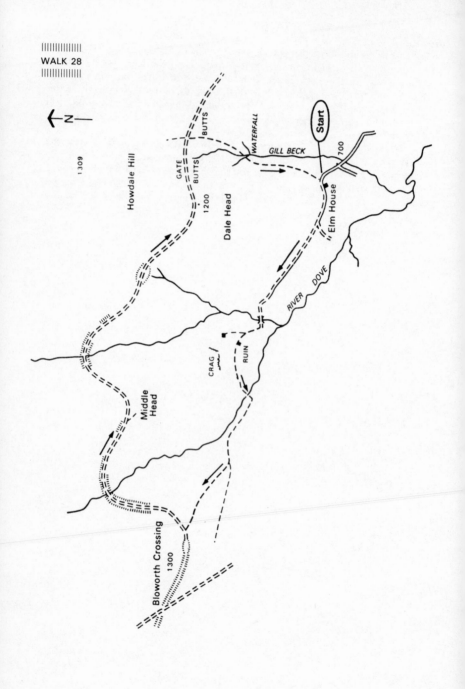

||||||||||||
WALK 28
||||||||||||

←N—

1 309

Howdale Hill

BUTTS

GATE
BUTTS
1200

WATERFALL

GILL BECK

Start

700

Dale Head

Elm House

RIVER DOVE

CRAG

RUIN

Middle
Head

Bloworth Crossing
1300

FARNDALE, A RAILWAY TRACK
AND GILL BECK

WALK 28

★

5 miles (8 km)

This is a splendid excursion starting at 700 ft above sea level and giving 2 miles of easy walking at a height above 1,200 ft, taking in two lovely valleys, with fast-flowing streams, on the way. Walking conditions are good, apart from some marshy sections, and at two points close attention must be paid to route finding.

Take the car to the head of Farndale on the east side by turning up the road marked 'Dale End Only' in Church Houses and continuing for nearly 3 miles. You will know you have reached your destination when you have descended a steep hill, passed over a stream (Gill Beck) and observed a signpost on the left 'Bridle Road to Bloworth'. Ascend the road to a suitable layby on the right by a public footpath sign just before the next left-hand bend, and park here, taking care not to obstruct the gate (GR 642 003).

Continue walking along the road, passing Elm House, where the macadam ends, and you find yourself first on a rough track and then on a fine green road. The crags of Middle Head appear ahead: we shall be passing below and to the left of them. The track passes through a gateway before a ravine. Descend left to the bridge. Up the other side, keep to the right of a fence, with the ravine now to your right. Bear left with the fence. Pass through a gateway in the wall ahead and to the right of a ruined building. Ignore the other building over to the right.

Bearing left past the ruined building you will find the track has now become a single path, easily found and keeping to the right of a wall. Below on the left you will see a footbridge. Follow the wall to where it ends at two gateposts, turn left and walk down the field to cross the infant river Dove by the bridge. This is a delightful picnic spot. Bear right on the clear path, which crosses some boggy patches and passes through two facing gateposts. Ahead of you, you will see a wall climbing the hillside away from you: the path keeps to the left of this, passes through the wall at a gap in it (fine view back down Farndale) and continues upwards, now with the wall on the left.

The clear path soon bears right away from the wall, and now you must pay great attention to route finding. As you ascend, you will see two gulleys to your right with a heathery tongue between them: you are going to cross the first of these and pass round the head of the second. So, continue climbing until you reach an indistinct fork, still on the steep part of the slope, perhaps 40 yards before the gradient eases (if you find the gradient easing off as you walk, you have gone too far). The clearer path is the one going straight up the hillside, but you want the right-hand contouring one, which becomes clear before you reach the gulley. Cross this, climb steeply out of it again, and now the path is very clear, passing above the top of the second gulley.

Now your guide is what looks like an earth rampart with rocks in it going away from you. Follow the line of this rampart up until it ends (you may find the path clearer on the left-hand side of it), then keep forward on the same line and in less than 100 yards you will hit the old railway track, a former mineral line which, chiefly in the 19th century, carried iron ore from Rosedale to Middlesborough. Bloworth Crossing is a short distance to the left, but we turn right along the track, good for stepping out and making up any lost time. There is no map reading to do for the next 2 miles. Notice the engineering of the high embankments, the cuttings and the curve of the line, contouring just below the tops of the moors. Looking right here and there, one is able to follow the route of the outward journey. On the left the rough peat hags show how tough the going would be but for the use of this old track.

After Dale Head there is a gate across the track. Now comes another piece of tricky route finding. Your objective is clear: the valley of Gill Beck down to the right, the difficulty is getting there. Continue on the railway track for about 300 yards past the gate, until you are immediately above a line of wooden shooting butts descending the slope on your right (a stony footpath also comes in from the left at this point). A narrow path descends towards the first butt, and indeed continues, not always very clear and sometimes boggy, down the line of butts to the second last wooden one (the very last one is made of stone), where it begins to bear right away from them, and opposite the last wooden one it heads down towards the ravine. Don't go too far down towards the steep part of the ravine, or you'll be in trouble. Cross a side stream and continue on the narrow path to ford the main stream and bear left on the clear, narrow path with the deep ravine to your left.

Now it's plain sailing! The path descends along the lip of the ravine to pass through a gate. Continue forward down the hollow way to pick up a wall which you keep to your left. Passing through another gate you are now between two walls. Follow the one on the left down to the road and your car.

ROSEDALE AND NORTHDALE

WALK 29

★

2½ miles (4 km)

Rosedale Abbey is a lovely little village situated at the confluence of the river Seven and Northdale Beck. The name of the village can be confusing because there is no abbey there, although a few fragments of a 12th century nunnery can be seen near the church.

Up the dale from the village are two very fine conical hills within the valley, each surmounted by a clump of conifers. The stroll now being suggested takes one up the main valley of the Seven for a short distance, cuts across to Northdale by way of a route between the two knolls, then returns beside Northdale Beck to the village. Northdale is a secluded, peaceful spot in which to linger.

The best approach to Rosedale from the south is via Pickering, Wrelton and Cropton. If coming from Kirkbymoorside, the direct approach via Hutton-le-Hole brings one down the one in three gradient of Rosedale Bank. The approaches from the north via Castleton or Egton Bridge are quite reasonable for the motorist, although the gradients are steep here and there, especially on the Egton Bridge road via Hamer House. Two free car parks are signposted in the village, near the main crossroads, one just above the Milburn Arms Hotel (off the Egton road), the other just below it (off the Castleton road). Park in one of these (GR 725 959).

Return to the crossroads and take the road opposite the one to Egton, walking past St Lawrence's church and Rosedale Abbey county primary school. Just past the school bear right and keep bearing right until you see two public footpath signs about 20 yards apart on the left. Cross the stile by the second sign and walk forward to turn right along the metalled drive (there is a children's playground on the left). Having entered the caravan site bear slightly left, pass to the right of the toilet block, and at the next fork in a few yards keep right (footpath sign); the road is signposted to Mill Dam and The Meadow. Just beyond a car park for visitors to the caravan site keep straight ahead to pass through a kissing-gate to the left of a large metal gate.

Walk along with the hedge/fence and caravan site to your left. Cross a stile in the far corner of the field and continue with the fence to your left. The bank beyond it is a mass of bluebells in May. Soon the fence ends and the clear path crosses the field, descending gently to cross another stile at the far end of the field into woodland. Keep ahead, ignoring the

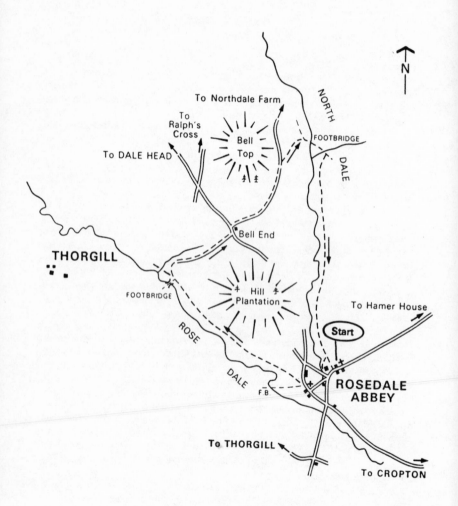

footbridge down on the left, but a few yards further on take the right fork, on a clear path which soon begins to climb. It bears right (the view back is attractive). After crossing a stile continue with the hedge to your right, the knoll left ahead is Bell Top, the one to your right is Hill Plantation, to reach the road at Bell End Farm.

Go left for a few yards, but at the end of the buildings turn right into a No Through Road which soon begins to climb a little and gives good views looking down the dale on the right. At a gate where the road begins to turn the corner of the hill you start to get views of Northdale. Keep on the road, passing through a gate and then dropping to pass through a gateway where a stream goes under the road from left to right. Ten yards further on take the green track forking right (public footpath sign), which leads down (lovely views ahead) to cross the delightful little beck by a stone footbridge.

Now some attention must be paid to route finding! Go through the facing gate and straight forward up the bank, keeping along the top edge of it until you are faced by a stream ahead. Turn left uphill with the stream to your right until you reach a bridle-gate in the wall on the right. Walk straight across the next field to the obvious gateway ahead, just to the left of a telegraph pole. Pass through, and ignoring the gateway at the far side of the next field, bear slightly right to pass under the telegraph wires and drop gently to a ladder-stile in the bottom corner of the field. Now bear slightly left, cross the field and ascend the bank ahead, then follow the top of the bank along until a few yards before a facing wall you bear right down the bank to cross this wall by a ladder-stile. The stream is to your right.

Walk straight across the next field to a step-stile among some large trees ahead, then keep along the fence/stream on your right to another step-stile at the end of the next field. Follow the beck on your right through another field, then the path goes across the next field (you are now further away from the beck) to a wooden stile at the right-hand end of the wall ahead. Continue by the beck, soon bearing slightly left to pass through a large gate. Cross straight over the next field, passing under the telegraph wires, to another stile beside a facing gate.

If you are parked in the lower car park you should now follow the track descending right. If in the upper one keep straight across the field, with a football pitch to your left, to pass through the facing gate into the car park.

WALK 30

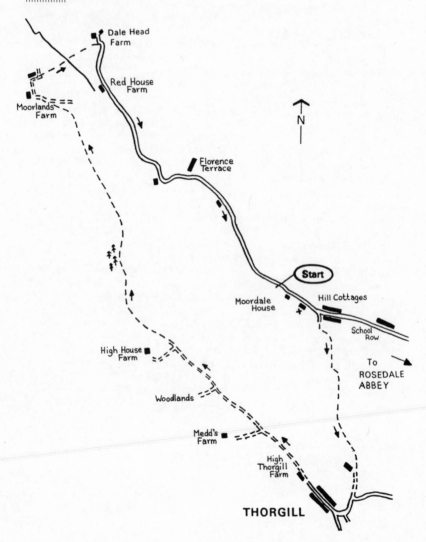

Dale Head Farm

Red House Farm

Moorlands Farm

Florence Terrace

N

Start

Moordale House

Hill Cottages

School Row

To ROSEDALE ABBEY

High House Farm

Woodlands

Medd's Farm

High Thorgill Farm

THORGILL

UPPER ROSEDALE

WALK 30

★

4 miles (6.5 km)

The history of Rosedale is bound up with the making of iron. In medieval times the discovery of rich deposits of iron ore made Cleveland a centre of the industry; the monks of Byland Abbey made iron in Rosedale from the mid 13th to the early 16th century. But it was in the mid 19th century that Rosedale became a centre of intensive industrial activity when the mineral railway to Battersby was engineered, for the transport of ore and iron blooms to the furnaces of Teesside. This went on into the early 20th century. The scars are still there in the form of ruins of old buildings, pits and ovens, but they have been mellowed by the passage of time, and one is left with a romantic picture of the days when the valley teemed with thousands of workmen, some of whose cottages are still in use, many as holiday homes, nicely painted and well preserved.

The old railway track offers fine possibilities for the walker. In Rosedale there are two tracks, the one from the east side contouring round the head of the valley to meet the west side track at Little Blakey. But our ramble today offers a more intimate view of the valley, a gentle stroll on clear tracks and paths through delightful and peaceful countryside.

Motor northwards from Rosedale Abbey up the dale towards Castleton for rather less than a mile when you come to a fork. Follow the left-hand road leading to 'Dale Head only', pass a row of cottages on the right (School Row) and between a row on each side of the road (Hill Cottages) (where there is a telephone kiosk), and a short distance further on you will pass a building which serves both as a Methodist church and as a field centre for Headlands School, and the red-painted Moordale House with a Queen Victoria post-box set into its wall, before coming to a layby on the left large enough for several cars. Park here (GR 707 977). If it is full, which is unlikely, there is other suitable roadside parking a little further on, but take care not to block gates.

Walk back the way you have come, and immediately before the row of cottages take the track on the right (footpath sign). In 100 yards it bears left, passes a row of garages, then bears right through a kissing-gate, drops gently to another kissing-gate then bears right down the middle of the next field to another kissing-gate beside a large gate in the gap in the hedge ahead. Continue straight down the middle of the next field, cross the footbridge and stile and follow the paved path across the next field to

95

another footbridge. Walk straight up the bank ahead to the marker post and over the field to join a track which passes between barns into the yard at Low Thorgill Farm. Bear left for a few yards then right up the farm access road.

When the track forks keep right and then bear right along the motor road through the lovely hamlet of Thorgill. Just after crossing a bridge there is an Edward VII post-box on the right. Follow the tarmacked road to its end, then keep on along the track. Some buildings at High Thorgill Farm have been converted into attractive holiday cottages. There are lovely views over the dale. Ignore a track forking left to Medd's Farm. Can you spot a section of old paved path to the right of the track? Just after a group of green caravans ('Seven Side') ignore a track forking left to Woodlands, and when the main track bears left to High House keep forward through the gate on a rather less well maintained track.

The track leads past a derelict farm and continues forward through a gateway, with a wall to the right. Just after passing a conifer wood on the left, pass through a gateway: the track forks. Keep right, on the better track, passing to the right of the small wood ahead. Pass through a gate and continue forward at first still with a wood to your left. Eventually you pass through a gateway and the track bears left as a hollowed way, following the wall on the left round to join the access road to Moorlands Farm. Turn left up to the farm. In the farmyard, with the house straight in front of you, bear right through a gate and continue along the track. Bear right down the side of the next set of buildings ahead, but when the track next turns left, cross the stile ahead between the two gates. Bear left down the field, bearing slightly right away from the wall on your left to drop down a shallow gulley you will see ahead at the foot of the field.

Cross the footbridge and bear right up the bank. Keep some yards to the left of the solitary power line pole and you will soon spot a gate at the far side of the field at the left-hand end of the trees, with Dale Head Farm up to the left. Pass through and keep forward, contouring near the bottom of the slope, with the beck to your right, to a footpath sign ahead. Turn right along the road to return to the car.